# Naming and Necessity

# NAMING AND NECESSITY

Saul A. Kripke

BLACKWELL PUBLISHING
350 Main Street, Malden, MA 02148-5020, USA
9600 Garsington Road, Oxford OX4 2DQ, UK
550 Swanston Street, Carlton, Victoria 3053, Australia



First published in G. Harman and D. Davidson (editors), *Semantics of Natural Language*
(D. Reidel Publishing Co., Dordrecht, Netherlands & Boston, USA, 1972)
Revised and enlarged edition first published 1980
Paperback edition 1981

32 2019

*Library of Congress Cataloging-in-Publication Data has been applied for*

ISBN 978-0-631-12801-4 (pbk: alk. paper)

A catalogue record for this title is available from the British Library.

Printed and bound in Singapore by
Markono Print Media Pte Ltd

The publisher's policy is to use permanent paper from mills that operate a sustainable forestry policy, and which has been manufactured from pulp processed using acid-free and elementary chlorine-free practices. Furthermore, the publisher ensures that the text paper and cover board used have met acceptable environmental accreditation standards.

For further information on
Blackwell Publishing, visit our website:
www.blackwellpublishing.com

*for*

MARGARET

# CONTENTS


| | |
|---|---|
| Preface | 1 |
| Lecture I | 22 |
| Lecture II | 71 |
| Lecture III | 106 |
| Addenda | 156 |

# PREFACE

Originally I had intended to revise or augment *Naming and Necessity* extensively. Considerable time has elapsed, and I have come to realize that any extensive revision or expansion would delay the appearance of a separate, less expensive edition of *Naming and Necessity* indefinitely. Further, as far as revision is concerned, there is something to be said for preserving a work in its original form, warts and all. I have thus followed a very conservative policy of correction for the present printing. Obvious printing errors have been corrected, and slight changes have been made to make various sentences or formulations clearer.[1] A good indication of my conservative policy is in footnote 56. In that footnote the letter-nomenclature for the various objects involved, inexplicably garbled in the original printing, has been corrected; but I make no mention of the fact that the argument of the footnote now seems to me to have problems which I did not know when I wrote it and which at least require further discussion.[2]

The same considerations lead me to give up any serious attempt to use this preface to amplify my previous argument, to fill in lacunae, or to deal with serious criticisms or difficulties.

[1] I thank Margaret Gilbert for her valuable help in this editing.

[2] Although I have not had time for careful study of Nathan Salmon's criticism (*Journal of Philosophy* (1979), pp. 703–25) of this footnote, it seems likely that his criticism of the argument, though related to mine, is not the same and reconstructs it in a way that does not correspond to my exact intent and makes the argument unnecessarily weak. Also, I think I had no ambition in this short footnote rigorously to prove 'essentialism from the theory of reference' alone. The footnote was so compressed that readers might easily reconstruct the details in differing ways.

Obviously, aside from such amplification in the preface, there are passages in the monograph other than just footnote 56 that I might modify. I do stand by the principal theses of my work, and the pressure for much revision is not intense. I will, however, use this preface briefly to describe the background and genesis of the leading ideas of this monograph, and to discuss a few misapprehensions that seem to be common. I am afraid that I must disappoint those readers who already found the exposition in the monograph satisfactory on these points. Relatively little will be added to deal with what I see as the more substantive problems of the monograph. The issues explained further—mostly related to modality and rigid designation—may already have been clear to most readers. On the other hand, those readers who felt sympathetic to some of the objections mentioned here may well be justified in wishing for a more thorough treatment. I fear that in most cases, the treatment of disputed points allowable in the space of a preface is simply too short to convince many readers who were inclined to believe the objections. To some extent, brief treatments of objections may do more harm than good, since the reader who was confused may think that if *this* is all that can be replied, the original objection must have been cogent. Nevertheless, I thought I should register briefly why I think certain reactions are misconceived. I hope that in some cases I will be able to write at greater length. Here I must plead that a thorough discussion is impossible within the bounds of this preface.[3]

Readers who are new to this book can use the preface for further clarification of certain points, and for a brief history of their genesis. I would recommend that such readers not read

[3] Thus some published criticisms are not discussed here because they are so frivolous that I hope they are not given wide credence; others because they are too substantive; and yet others simply for lack of space. I leave it to the reader to decide which category subsumes any particular example.

the preface first, but that they return to it for clarification (if necessary) after they have read the main text. The preface is *not* written in such a way as to be completely self-contained.

The ideas in *Naming and Necessity* evolved in the early sixties —most of the views were formulated in about 1963–64. Of course the work grew out of earlier formal work in the model theory of modal logic. Already when I worked on modal logic it had seemed to me, as Wiggins has said, that the Leibnitzian principle of the indiscernibility of identicals[4] was as self-evident as the law of contradiction. That some philosophers could have doubted it always seemed to me bizarre. The model theoretic study of modal logic ('possible worlds' semantics) could only confirm this conviction—the alleged counter-examples involving modal properties always turned out to turn on some confusion: the contexts involved did not express genuine properties, scopes were confused, or coincidence between individual concepts was confused with identity between individuals. The model theory made this completely clear, though it should have been clear enough on the intuitive level. Waiving fussy considerations deriving from the fact that $x$ need not have necessary existence, it was clear from $(x) \Box (x = x)$ and Leibnitz's law that identity is an 'internal' relation: $(x)(y)(x = y \supset \Box\, x = y)$. (What pairs $(x, y)$ could be counter-examples? Not pairs of distinct objects, for then the antecedent is false; nor any pair of an object and itself, for then the consequent is true.) If '*a*' and '*b*' are rigid designators, it follows that '$a = b$', if true, is a necessary truth. If '*a*' and '*b*' are *not* rigid designators, no such conclusion follows about the *statement* '$a = b$' (though the *objects* designated by '*a*' and '*b*' will be necessarily identical).

In speaking of rigid designators, we are speaking of a

[4] The principle that identicals have all properties in common; schematically, $(x)(y)(x = y \wedge Fx. \supset. Fy)$. Not to be confused with the identity of indiscernibles.

possibility that certainly exists in a formal modal language. Logically, we as yet are committed to no thesis about the status of what we ordinarily call 'names' in natural language. We must distinguish three distinct theses: (i) that identical objects are necessarily identical; (ii) that true identity statements between rigid designators are necessary; (iii) that identity statements between what we call 'names' in actual language are necessary. (i) and (ii) are (self-evident) theses of philosophical logic independent of natural language. They are related to each other, though (i) is about objects and (ii) is metalinguistic. ((ii) roughly 'follows' from (i), using substitution of rigid designators for universal quantifiers—I say 'roughly' because delicate distinctions about rigidity are relevant, see page 21 n. 21; the analogous deduction for nonrigid designators is fallacious.) From (ii) all that strictly follows about so-called 'names' in natural language is that *either* they are not rigid *or* true identities between them are necessary. Our intuitive idea of naming suggests that names are rigid, but I suppose that at one time I vaguely supposed, influenced by prevailing presuppositions, that since obviously there are contingent identities between ordinary so-called names, such ordinary names must not be rigid. However, it was already clear from (i)—without any investigation of natural language—that the supposition, common to philosophical discussions of materialism at that time, that *objects* can be 'contingently identical', is false. Identity would be an internal relation even if natural language had contained no rigid designators. The confused reference to objects as 'contingently identical' served illegitimately as a philosophical crutch: It enabled philosophers *simultaneously* to think of certain designators as if they were non-rigid (and hence found in 'contingent identities') *and* as if they were rigid, the conflict being muddled over by thinking of the corresponding *objects* as 'contingently identical'. Even before I clearly realized the true situation regarding proper names, I felt little sympathy for the dark doctrine of a relation of 'contingent identity'. Uniquely identifying properties can coincide contingently, but objects cannot be 'contingently identical'.

Eventually I came to realize—this realization inaugurated the aforementioned work of 1963–64—that the received presuppositions against the necessity of identities between ordinary names were incorrect, that the natural intuition that the names of ordinary language are rigid designators can in fact be upheld.[5] Part of the effort to make this clear involved the distinction between using a description to give a meaning and using it to fix a reference. Thus at this stage I rejected the conventional description theory as an account of meaning, though its validity as an account of the fixing of a reference was left untouched. Probably I let myself be content with this position momentarily, but the natural next step was to question whether the description theory gave a correct account even of how the references of names were fixed. The result appears in the second of these lectures. It was a short step to realize that similar remarks applied to terms for natural kinds. The other leading ideas came naturally as things 'fit into place'.

Let me not pay inadequate tribute to the power of the then prevailing complex of ideas, emanating from Frege and from Russell, that I then abandoned. The natural and uniform manner by which these ideas appear to account for a variety of philosophical problems—their marvelous internal coherence—is adequate explanation for their long appeal. I myself have been shocked at the prevalence of some ideas in the philosophical community which to me have little or no appeal, but I have never placed the description theory of proper names in such a category. Although I, with others, always felt some strain in this edifice, it took some time to get free of its seductive power.

[5] It also became clear that a symbol of any actual or hypothetical language that is *not* a rigid designator is so unlike the names of ordinary language that it ought not to be called a 'name'. In particular, this would apply to a hypothetical abbreviation of a nonrigid definite description.

Although the idea is now a familiar one, I will give a brief restatement of the idea of rigid designation, and the intuition about names that underlies it. Consider:

(1) Aristotle was fond of dogs.

A proper understanding of this statement involves an understanding both of the (extensionally correct) conditions under which it is in fact true, *and* of the conditions under which a counterfactual course of history, resembling the actual course in some respects but not in others, would be correctly (partially) described by (1). Presumably everyone agrees that there is a certain man—the philosopher we call 'Aristotle'—such that, as a matter of fact, (1) is true if and only if *he* was fond of dogs.[6] The thesis of rigid designation is simply—subtle points aside[7]—that the same paradigm applies to the truth conditions of (1) as it describes *counterfactual* situations. That is, (1) truly describes a counterfactual situation if and only if the same aforementioned man would have been fond of dogs, had that situation obtained. (Forget the counterfactual situations where he would not have existed.) By contrast, Russell thinks that (1) should be analyzed as something like:[8]

[6] That is everyone, even Russell, would agree that this is a true material equivalence, given that there really was an Aristotle.

[7] In particular, we ignore the question what to say about counterfactual situations in which Aristotle would not have existed. See page 21 note 21.

[8] Taking 'the last great philosopher of antiquity' to be the description Russell associates with 'Aristotle'. Let admirers of Epicureanism, Stoicism, etc., not be offended; if any reader thinks that someone later than Aristotle is the true referent of the description given, let that reader substitute another one.

I assume Russell is right in that definite descriptions can at least *sometimes* be interpreted nonrigidly. As I mention on page 59 footnote 22, some philosophers think that, in addition, there is a rigid sense of definite descriptions. As I say in the latter footnote, I am not convinced of this, but if these philosophers are right, my principal thesis is not affected. It contrasts names with nonrigid descriptions, as advocated by Russell. See Section 2, pp. 258–61 of my paper, 'Speaker's Reference and Semantic Reference', *Midwest Studies in Philosophy*, II (1977), pp. 255–76; also in *Contemporary Perspectives in the Philosophy of Language*, edited by Peter A. French, Theodore E. Uehling,

(2) The last great philosopher of antiquity was fond of dogs,

and that this in turn should be analyzed as

(3) Exactly one person was last among the great philosophers of antiquity, and any such person was fond of dogs.

The actual truth conditions of (3) agree extensionally with those mentioned above for (1), assuming that Aristotle was the last great philosopher of antiquity. But counterfactually, Russell's conditions can vary wildly from those supposed by the rigidity thesis. With respect to a counterfactual situation where someone other than Aristotle would have been the last great philosopher of antiquity, Russell's criterion would make *that other person's* fondness for dogs the relevant issue for the correctness of (1)!

So far I have said nothing that I did not think I had made clear before. But it should be apparent from the explanation that some criticisms are misunderstandings. Some have thought that the simple fact that two people can have the same name refutes the rigidity thesis. It is true that in the present monograph I spoke for simplicity as if each name had a unique bearer. I do not in fact think, as far as the issue of rigidity is concerned, that this is a major oversimplification. I believe that many important theoretical issues about the semantics of names (probably not all) would be largely unaffected had our conventions required that no two things shall be given the same name. In particular, as I shall explain, the issue of rigidity would be unaffected.

For language as we have it, we could speak of names as having a unique referent if we adopted a terminology, anal-

---

Jr., and Howard K. Wettstein, University of Minnesota Press, Minneapolis (1979), pp. 6–27) for a brief discussion of the relation of the idea of rigid definite descriptions to Donnellan's 'referential' descriptions. I also discuss the relation of both of these to the notion of scope.

ogous to the practice of calling homonyms distinct 'words', according to which uses of phonetically the same sounds to name distinct objects count as distinct names.[9] This terminology certainly does not agree with the most common usage,[10] but I think it may have a great deal to recommend it for theoretical purposes.

But the main point is that, however a philosophical theory may treat such 'homonymous'[11] names, the issue is irrelevant to the question of rigidity. As a speaker of my idiolect, I call only one object 'Aristotle', though I am aware that other people, including the man I call 'Onassis' or perhaps 'Aristotle Onassis', had the same given name. Other readers may use 'Aristotle' to name more than one object (person, or pet animal) and for them (1) has no unambiguous truth conditions. When I spoke of 'the truth conditions' of (1), I perforce assumed a particular reading for (1). (So of course, does the classical description theorist; *this* is not an issue between us. Classical description theorists, too, tended to speak for simplicity as if names had

[9] Actually, the criterion should be subtler, and depends on one's theoretical views. Thus, on the picture advocated in this monograph, two totally distinct 'historical chains' that by sheer accident assign phonetically the same name to the same man should probably count as creating distinct names despite the identity of the referents. The identity may well be unknown to the speaker, or express a recent discovery. (Similarly, a description theorist who counts names in the way suggested presumably would regard two phonetically identical names with distinct associated descriptions as distinct, even if the two descriptions happen uniquely to be true of the same object.) But distinctness of the referents will be a *sufficient* condition for distinctness of the names.

I should stress that I am not demanding or even advocating this usage, but mention it as a possibility to which I am sympathetic. The point that rigidity has nothing to do with the question of two people having phonetically the same name holds whether this convention is adopted or not.

[10] But perhaps one use of 'How many names are there in this telephone book?' is an exception (Anne Jacobson).

[11] By using this term, I do not mean to *commit* the analysis to a particular view (see also the next footnote), though I *suggest* my own. I mean simply that two people can have phonetically the same name.

unique references.) In practice it is usual to suppose that what is meant in a particular use of a sentence is understood from the context. In the present instance, that context made it clear that it was the conventional use of 'Aristotle' for the great philosopher that was in question. Then, *given* this fixed understanding of (1), the question of rigidity is: Is the correctness of (1), *thus understood*, determined with respect to each counterfactual situation by whether a certain single person would have liked dogs (had that situation obtained)? I answer the question affirmatively. But Russell seems to be committed to the opposite view, even when what (1) expresses is fixed by the context. Only given such a fixed understanding of (1) would Russell read (1) as (3)—not if 'Aristotle' meant Onassis!—but the rigidity requirement is violated. This question is entirely unaffected by the presence or absence in the language of other readings of (1). For each such particular reading separately, we can ask whether what is expressed would be true of a counterfactual situation if and only if some fixed individual has the appropriate property. *This* is the question of rigidity.

Let me recapitulate the point, ignoring for this exposition the delicate problems about 'propositions' to be mentioned at the end of this preface. To speak of 'the truth conditions' of a sentence such as (1), it must be taken to express a *single* proposition—otherwise its truth conditions even with respect to the actual world are indeterminate. Thus ambiguous words or homonyms (perhaps 'dog' in (1)) must be read in a determinate way (canine!), indexicals must be assigned determinate references, syntactic ambiguities must be resolved, and it must be fixed whether 'Aristotle' names the philosopher or the shipping magnate. Only *given* such a reading can Russell propose an analysis such as (3)—rightly, no one ever faulted him on this score. Then my objection to Russell is that all the many propositions expressed by various readings of (1) (assuming that in all readings 'Aristotle' is a proper name) would, if he were right, fail to conform to the rule of rigidity. That is, no such proposition conforms to the rule that there is a single individual and a single property such that, with respect to every counterfactual situation, the truth conditions of the proposition are the possession of the property by that individual, in that situation. (I am relying on the fact that in practice Russell invariably interprets ordinary names nonrigidly.) That more than one proposition may be expressed by (1) is irrelevant: the question is whether each such proposition is evaluated as I describe, or is it not. The view applies to each such proposition taken separately. Detailed questions as to how the theory should incorporate the fact that our linguistic practice allows two things to have phonetically the same name need not be settled for this to be clear.[12]

Another misconception concerns the relation of rigidity to scope, which apparently I treated too briefly. It seems often to be supposed that all the linguistic intuitions I adduce on behalf of rigidity could just as well be handled by reading names in various sentences as nonrigid designators with wide scopes, analogously to wide scope descriptions. It would, indeed, be possible to interpret *some* of these intuitions as results of scope ambiguities instead of rigidity—this I recognize in the monograph. To this extent the objection is justified, but it seems to me to be wrong to suppose that *all* our intuitions can be handled in this way. I dealt with the question rather briefly, on page 62 and in the accompanying footnote 25, but the discussion seems to have been overlooked by many readers. In the footnote I

[12] For example, some philosophers would assimilate proper names to demonstratives. Their reference varies from utterance to utterance the way that of a demonstrative does. This does not affect the issues discussed, since the reference of a demonstrative must be given for a definite proposition to be expressed. Although I did not discuss the question in the present monograph, of course it was part of my view (p. 49 n. 16) that 'this', 'I', 'you', etc., are all rigid (even though their references obviously vary with the context of utterance). The rigidity of demonstratives has been stressed by David Kaplan.

adduce some linguistic phenomena that, I think, support the rigidity intuition as opposed to an explanation in terms of scope. Many of these readers even seem to have overlooked the intuitive test for rigidity, as emphasized on pages 48–49. I will not repeat or elaborate these considerations in this preface, even though they seem to have been stated too briefly. Exigencies of a preface may make the following remarks too brief as well, but I shall discuss the scope question in the light of the present explanation of rigidity.

It has even been asserted that my own view itself reduces to a view about scope, that the doctrine of rigidity simply *is* the doctrine that natural language has a convention that a name, in the context of any sentence, should be read with a large scope including all modal operators.[13] This latter idea is particularly wide of the mark; in terms of modal logic, it represents a technical error. Let me deal with it first. (1) and (2) are 'simple' sentences. Neither contains modal or other operators, so there is no room for any scope distinctions.[14] No scope convention about more complex sentences affects the interpretation of *these* sentences. Yet the issue of rigidity makes

[13] See Michael Dummett, *Frege* (Duckworth, 1973), p. 128. Unfortunately, many of Dummett's other ideas or remarks on the relation of rigidity to scope are technically erroneous—for example, on the same page he says that I hold that descriptions are never (?) rigid and equates this view with the claim that 'within a modal context, the scope of a definite description should always be taken to exclude the modal operator.' Also, some of his comments on linguistic intuitions seem to me to be in error. I cannot deal with these matters here.

[14] Actually the sentences in question are tensed and therefore can be interpreted in a formal language with tense operators. If we treat tense this way (it can be treated in other ways), then other scope questions can arise owing to the *tense* operators. The question at issue, however, is about the relation of scope to *modal* operators, which does not arise in these sentences even if tense operators are used in their analysis. The assertion that the sentences in question give rise to no scope questions can be made literally true either by treating tense without using operators or (better) by taking the copula in (1) and (2) to be tenseless.

sense as applied to both. My view is that 'Aristotle' in (1) is rigid, but 'the last great philosopher of antiquity' in (2) is not. No hypothesis about scope conventions for modal contexts expresses this view;[15] it is a doctrine about the truth conditions, with respect to counterfactual situations, of (the propositions expressed by) *all* sentences, including *simple* sentences.

This shows that the view that *reduces* rigidity to scope in the manner stated is simply in error. It also indicates one weakness of the (rather more understandable) reaction that attempts to use scope to *replace* rigidity. The doctrine of rigidity supposes that a painting or picture purporting to represent a situation correctly described by (1) must *ipso facto* purport to depict Aristotle himself as fond of dogs. No picture, purporting to represent someone else and his fondness for dogs, even if it depicts the other individual as possessing all the properties we use to identify Aristotle, represents a counterfactual situation correctly described by (1). Doesn't this, in itself, obviously represent our intuitions regarding (1)? The intuition is about the truth conditions, in counterfactual situations, of (the proposition expressed by) a *simple* sentence. No wide-scope interpretation of certain modal contexts can take its place. To the extent that a theory preserves this intuition, so much the better for it.

Another remark, not so directly relying on counterfactual situations, may illuminate matters. In the monograph I argued that the truth conditions of 'It might have been the case that Aristotle was fond of dogs' conform to the rigidity theory: no proof that some person *other* than Aristotle might have been

[15] The thesis that names are rigid in simple sentences is, however, equivalent (ignoring complications arising from the possible nonexistence of the object) to the thesis that if a modal operator governs a simple sentence containing a name, the two readings with large and small scopes are equivalent. This is *not* the same as the doctrine that natural language has a convention that only the large scope reading is allowed. In fact, the equivalence makes sense only for a language where both readings are admissible.

both fond of dogs and the greatest philosopher of antiquity is relevant to the truth of the quoted statement. The situation is unchanged if we replace 'the greatest philosopher of antiquity' by any other (nonrigid) definite description thought of as identifying Aristotle. Similarly, I held, 'It might have been the case that Aristotle was not a philosopher' expresses a truth, though 'It might have been the case that the greatest philosopher of antiquity was not a philosopher' does not, contrary to Russell's theory. (An analogous example could be given for any other nonrigid identifying description.) Now the last quoted sentence would express a truth if the description used were read, contrary to my intent, with wide scope. So perhaps it might be supposed that the problem simply arises from an (unaccountable!) tendency to give 'Aristotle' a wide scope reading while the descriptions are given a small scope reading; sentences with both names and descriptions, however, would be subject in principle to both readings. My point, however, was that the contrast would hold if all the sentences involved were explicitly construed with small scopes (perhaps by inserting a colon after 'that'). Further, I gave examples (referred to above) to indicate that the situation with names was not in fact parallel to that with large scope descriptions. Proponents of the contrary view often seem to have overlooked these examples, but this is not my point here. The contrary view must hold that our language and thought are, somehow, impotent to keep the distinction straight, that it is this which is responsible for the difficulty. It is hard to see how this can be: how did we make the distinction if we cannot make it? If the formulation with a that clause really is so tangled that we are unable to distinguish one reading of it from another, what about:

(4) What (1) expresses might have been the case.

Doesn't this express the desired assertion, with no scope ambiguities? If not, what would do so? (The formulation might be a bit more natural in a dialogue: 'Aristotle was fond of dogs.' 'That's not the case, though it might have been.') Now my claim is that our understanding of (4) conforms to the theory of rigidity. No possible situation in which anyone but Aristotle himself was fond of dogs can be relevant.

My main remark, then, is that we have a direct intuition of the rigidity of names, exhibited in our understanding of the truth conditions of particular sentences. In addition, various secondary phenomena, about 'what we would say', such as the ones I mention in the monograph and others, give indirect evidence of rigidity. How did Russell, for one, propose a theory plainly incompatible with our direct intuitions of rigidity? One reason is that, here as elsewhere, he did not consider modal questions; and the question of the rigidity of names in natural language was rarely explicitly considered after him. Second, it seemed to Russell that various philosophical arguments necessitated a description theory of names and an eliminative theory of descriptions. Russell acknowledged that his views were incompatible with our naive reactions (though the rigidity issue was not mentioned), but powerful philosophical arguments seemed to him to compel adoption of his theory. Regarding the question of rigidity, my own reply took the form of a thought experiment, along the lines sketched briefly for 'identity and schmidentity' on page 108 of the present monograph. In the present case I imagined a hypothetical formal language in which a rigid designator '*a*' is introduced with the ceremony, 'Let "*a*" (rigidly) denote the unique object that actually has property *F*, when talking about any situation, actual or counterfactual.' It seemed clear that if a speaker did introduce a designator into a language that way, then in virtue of his very linguistic act, he would be in a position to say 'I know that *Fa*', but nevertheless '*Fa*' would express a contingent truth (provided that *F* is not an essential property of the unique object that possesses it). First, this showed that epistemic questions should be separated from questions of necessity and contingency, and that to fix a reference is not to give a synonym. More important, this situation indicated that the evidence ordinarily adduced to show that names were synonymous with descriptions could instead be rationalized by this hypothetical model. In addition, the model satisfied our intuitions of rigidity. Given this, the burden of the argument seemed to fall heavily on the philosopher who wished to deny our natural intuition of rigidity. As I said above, the further observation that ordinarily speakers do not even fix references by identifying descriptions of the usual type came later.

I will say something briefly about 'possible worlds'.[16] (I hope to elaborate elsewhere.) In the present monograph I argued against those misuses of the concept that regard possible worlds as something like distant planets, like our own surroundings but somehow existing in a different dimension, or that lead to spurious problems of 'transworld identification'. Further, if one wishes to avoid the *Weltangst* and philosophical confusions that many philosophers have associated with the 'worlds' terminology, I recommended that 'possible state (or history) of the world', or 'counterfactual situation' might be better. One should even remind oneself that the 'worlds' terminology can often be replaced by modal talk—'It is possible that . . .'

[16] Some of the worst misinterpretations of rigidity would have had much less currency if the relevant philosophical discussions had been conducted in the context of a rigorous presentation in terms of 'possible worlds semantics'. I did not do this in the present monograph both because I did not wish to rest the argument heavily on a formal model and because I wished the presentation to be philosophical rather than technical. To readers who are thoroughly familiar with intensional semantics the rough outline of a presentation of my views in these terms should be clear without an explicit development. Nevertheless, some misunderstandings of the rigidity concept—including some aspects of these mentioned in this preface—led me to think that a technical presentation might eliminate some misconceptions. Eventually considerations of time and space led me to decide against including such material, but I may give such a formal exposition elsewhere.

But I do not wish to leave any exaggerated impression that I repudiate possible worlds altogether, or even that I regard them as a mere formal device. My own use of them should have been extensive enough to preclude any such misunderstanding. In fact, there are some conceptions of 'possible worlds' that I repudiate and some I do not. An analogy from school—in fact, it is not merely an analogy—will help to clarify my view. Two ordinary dice (call them die A and die B) are thrown, displaying two numbers face up. For each die, there are six possible results. Hence there are thirty-six possible states of the pair of dice, as far as the numbers shown face-up are concerned, though only one of these states corresponds to the way the dice actually will come out. We all learned in school how to compute the probabilities of various events (assuming equiprobability of the states). For example, since there are just two states—(die A, 5; die B, 6) and (die A, 6; die B, 5)—that yield a total throw of eleven, the probability of throwing eleven is $2/36 = 1/18$.

Now in doing these school exercises in probability, we were in fact introduced at a tender age to a set of (miniature) 'possible worlds'. The thirty-six possible states of the dice are literally thirty-six 'possible worlds', as long as we (fictively) ignore everything about the world except the two dice and what they show (and ignore the fact that one or both dice might not have existed). Only one of these miniworlds—the one corresponding to the way the dice in fact come up—is the 'actual world', but the others are of interest when we ask how probable or improbable the actual outcome was (or will be). Now in this elementary case, certain confusions can be avoided. We have assumed that the dice actually do fall, that some one of the thirty-six states is actual. Now the 'actual world' in this case is the *state* of the dice that is actually realized. *Another* entity, more 'concrete' than this state, is the Lesniewskian-Goodmanian physical entity which is the 'sum' of the two dice. This complex physical entity ('the dice,' thought of as a single object) is before me on the table, after the throw, and its actual position determines the actual state of the (two) dice. But when we talk in school of thirty-six possibilities, in no way do we need to posit that there are some thirty-five *other* entities, existent in some never-never land, corresponding to the physical object before me. Nor need we ask whether these phantom entities are composed of (phantom) 'counterparts' of the actual individual dice, or are somehow composed of the same individual dice themselves but in 'another dimension'. The thirty-six possibilities, the one that is actual included, are (abstract) *states* of the dice, not complex physical entities. Nor should any school pupil receive high marks for the question 'How do we know, in the state where die A is six and die B is five, whether it is die A or die B which is six? Don't we need a "criterion of transstate identity" to identify the die with a six—not the die with a five—with our die A?' The answer is, of course, that the state (die A, 6; die B, 5) is *given* as such (and distinguished from the state (die B, 6; die A, 5)). The demand for some further 'criterion of transstate identity' is so confused that no competent schoolchild would be so perversely philosophical as to make it. The 'possibilities' simply are not given purely qualitatively (as in: one die, 6, the other, 5). If they had been, there would have been just twenty-one distinct possibilities, not thirty-six. And the states are not phantom dice-pairs, viewed from afar, about which we can raise epistemically meaningful questions of the form, 'Which die is that?' Nor, when we regard such qualitatively identical states as (A, 6; B, 5) and (A, 5; B, 6) as distinct, need we suppose that A and B are qualitatively distinguishable in some other respect, say, color. On the contrary, for the purposes of the probability problem, the numerical face shown is thought of as if it were the only property of each die. Finally, in setting up this innocent little exercise regarding the fall of the dice, with possibilities that are not described purely qualitatively, we make no obscure metaphysical commitment to dice as 'bare particulars', whatever that might mean.[17]

'Possible worlds' are little more than the miniworlds of school probability blown large. It is true that there are problems in the general notion not involved in the miniature version. The miniature worlds are tightly controlled, both as to the objects involved (two dice), the relevant properties (number on face shown), and (thus) the relevant idea of possibility. 'Possible worlds' are total 'ways the world might have been', or states or histories of the *entire* world. To think of the totality of all of them involves much more idealization, and more mind-boggling questions, than the less ambitious elementary school analogue. Certainly the philosopher of 'possible worlds' must take care that his technical apparatus not push him to ask questions whose meaningfulness is not supported by our original intuitions of possibility that gave the apparatus its point. Further, in practice we cannot describe a complete counterfactual course of events and have no need to do so. A practical description of the extent to which the 'counterfactual situation' differs in the relevant way from the actual facts is sufficient; the 'counterfactual situation' could be thought of as a miniworld or a ministate, restricted to features of the world relevant to the problem at hand. In practice this involves less idealization both as to considering entire world histories and as to considering *all* possibilities. For present purposes, however, the elementary analogue gives a fine model for the

[17] With respect to possible states of the entire world, I do not mean to assert categorically that, just as in the case of the dice, there are qualitatively identical but distinct (counterfactual) states. What I do assert is that *if* there is a philosophical argument excluding qualitatively identical but distinct worlds, it cannot be based simply on the supposition that worlds must be stipulated purely qualitatively. What I defend is the *propriety* of giving possible worlds in terms of certain particulars as well as qualitatively, whether or not there are in fact qualitatively identical but distinct worlds.

appropriate morals regarding 'possible worlds'. There is nothing wrong in principle with taking these, for philosophical or for technical purposes, as (abstract) entities—the innocence of the grammar school analogue should allay any anxieties on that score.[18] (Indeed the general notion of 'sample space' that forms the basis of modern probability theory is just that of such a space of possible worlds.) However, we should avoid the pitfalls that seem much more tempting to philosophers with their grand worlds than to schoolchildren with their modest versions. There are no special grounds to suppose that possible worlds must be given qualitatively, or that there need be any genuine problem of 'transworld identification'—the fact that larger and more complex states are involved than in the case of the dice makes no difference to this point. The 'actual world'—better, the actual state, or history of the world —should not be confused with the enormous scattered object

[18] I do not think of 'possible worlds' as providing a *reductive* analysis in any philosophically significant sense, that is, as uncovering the ultimate nature, from either an epistemological or a metaphysical point of view, of modal operators, propositions, etc., or as 'explicating' them. In the actual development of our thought, judgments involving directly expressed modal locutions ('it might have been the case that') certainly come earlier. The notion of a 'possible world', though it has its roots in various ordinary ideas of ways the world might have been, comes at a much greater, and subsequent, level of abstraction. In practice, no one who cannot understand the idea of possibility is likely to understand that of a 'possible world' either. Philosophically, we by no means need assume that one type of discourse is 'prior to' the other, independently of the purposes at hand. The main and the original motivation for the 'possible worlds analysis'—and the way it clarified modal logic—was that it enabled modal logic to be treated by the same set theoretic techniques of model theory that proved so successful when applied to extensional logic. It is also useful in making certain concepts clear.

To reiterate another point: the notion of *all* states of the entire world that are possible in the broadest (metaphysical) sense involves a certain amount of idealization, as well as philosophical questions I have not discussed. If we restrict the worlds to a narrower class of miniworlds, essentially all the issues regarding say, rigid designators, remain the same. So do the questions of modal semantics.

that surrounds us. The latter might also have been called 'the (actual) world', but it is not the relevant object here. Thus the possible but not actual worlds are not phantom duplicates of the 'world' in this other sense. Perhaps such confusions would have been less likely but for the terminological accident that 'possible worlds' rather than 'possible states', or 'histories', of the world, or 'counterfactual situations' had been used. Certainly they would have been avoided had philosophers adhered to the common practices of schoolchildren and probabilists.[19]

A final issue: Some critics of my doctrines, and some sympathizers, seem to have read them as asserting, or at least implying, a doctrine of the universal substitutivity of proper names. This can be taken as saying that a sentence with 'Cicero' in it expresses the same 'proposition' as the corresponding one with 'Tully', that to believe the proposition expressed by the one is to believe the proposition expressed by the other, or that they are equivalent for all semantic purposes. Russell does seem to have held such a view for 'logically proper names', and it seems congenial to a purely 'Millian' picture of naming, where only the referent of the name contributes to what is expressed. But I (and for all I know, even Mill[20]) never intended to go so far. My view that the English sentence 'Hesperus is Phosphorus' could sometimes be used to raise an empirical issue while 'Hesperus is Hesperus' could not shows that I do not treat the *sentences* as completely interchangeable. Further, it indicates that the mode of fixing the reference is relevant to our epistemic

[19] Compare, e.g., the 'moderate realism' regarding possible worlds of Robert Stalnaker, 'Possible Worlds', *Noûs*, vol. 10 (1976), pp. 65–75.

[20] Michael Lockwood ('On Predicating Proper Names', *The Philosophical Review*, vol. 84, no. 4, October, 1975, pp. 471–498) points out (p. 491) that Mill does *not* take 'Cicero is Tully' to mean the same as 'Cicero is Cicero' but rather holds the view that it means that 'Cicero' and 'Tully' are codesignative. He also points out (p. 490) that Mill sees such a metalinguistic component in all assertions involving names. I have not investigated the interpretation of Mill further, so I have no view as to his exact doctrine.

attitude toward the sentences expressed. How this relates to the question what 'propositions' are expressed by these sentences, whether these 'propositions' are objects of knowledge and belief, and in general, how to treat names in epistemic contexts, are vexing questions. I have no 'official doctrine' concerning them, and in fact I am unsure that the apparatus of 'propositions' does not break down in this area.[21] Hence, I sidestepped such questions; no firm doctrine regarding the point should be read into my words.

[21] Reasons why I find these questions so vexing are to be found in my 'A Puzzle About Belief', in *Meaning and Use* (ed. A. Margalit), Reidel, 1979, pp. 239–283. Of course there may be more than one notion of 'proposition', depending on the demands we make of the notion. The thesis of rigidity does of course imply interchangeability of codesignative names in *modal* contexts, subject to the usual caveat about possible nonexistence.

Concerning rigidity: In many places, both in this preface and in the text of this monograph, I deliberately ignore delicate questions arising from the possible nonexistence of an object. I also ignore the distinction between '*de jure*' rigidity, where the reference of a designator is *stipulated* to be a single object, whether we are speaking of the actual world or of a counterfactual situation, and mere '*de facto*' rigidity, where a description 'the $x$ such that $Fx$' happens to use a predicate '$F$' that in each possible world is true of one and the same unique object (e.g., 'the smallest prime' rigidly designates the number two). Clearly my thesis about names is that they are rigid *de jure*, but in the monograph I am content with the weaker assertion of rigidity. Since names are rigid *de jure*—see p. 78 below—I say that a proper name rigidly designates its referent even when we speak of counterfactual situations where that referent would not have existed. Thus the issues about nonexistence are affected. Various people have persuaded me that all these questions deserve a more careful discussion than I gave them in the monograph, but I must leave them here.

# LECTURE I: JANUARY 20, 1970[1]

I hope that some people see some connection between the two topics in the title. If not, anyway, such connections will be developed in the course of these talks. Furthermore, because of the use of tools involving reference and necessity in analytic philosophy today, our views on these topics really have wide-

[1] In January of 1970, I gave three talks at Princeton University transcribed here. As the style of the transcript makes clear, I gave the talks without a written text, and, in fact, without notes. The present text is lightly edited from the *verbatim* transcript; an occasional passage has been added to expand the thought, an occasional sentence has been rewritten, but no attempt has been made to change the informal style of the original. Many of the footnotes have been added to the original, but a few were originally spoken asides in the talks themselves.

I hope the reader will bear these facts in mind as he reads the text. Imagining it spoken, with proper pauses and emphases, may occasionally facilitate comprehension. I have agreed to publish the talks in this form with some reservations. The time allotted, and the informal style, necessitated a certain amount of compression of the argument, inability to treat certain objections, and the like. Especially in the concluding sections on scientific identities and the mind-body problem thoroughness had to be sacrificed. Some topics essential to a full presentation of the viewpoint argued here, especially that of existence statements and empty names, had to be omitted altogether. Further, the informality of the presentation may well have engendered a sacrifice of clarity at certain points. All these defects were accepted in the interest of early publication. I hope that perhaps I will have the chance to do a more thorough job later. To repeat, I hope the reader will bear in mind that he is largely reading informal lectures, not only when he encounters repetitions or infelicities, but also when he encounters irreverence or corn.

ranging implications for other problems in philosophy that traditionally might be thought far-removed, like arguments over the mind-body problem or the so-called 'identity thesis'. Materialism, in this form, often now gets involved in very intricate ways in questions about what is necessary or contingent in identity of properties—questions like that. So, it is really very important to philosophers who may want to work in many domains to get clear about these concepts. Maybe I will say something about the mind-body problem in the course of these talks. I want to talk also at some point (I don't know if I can get it in) about substances and natural kinds.

The way I approach these matters will be, in some ways, quite different from what people are thinking today (though it also has some points of contact with what some people have been thinking and writing today, and if I leave people out in informal talks like this, I hope that I will be forgiven).[2] Some of the views that I have are views which may at first glance strike some as obviously wrong. My favorite example is this (which I probably won't defend in the lectures—for one thing it doesn't ever convince anyone): It is a common claim in contemporary philosophy that there are certain predicates which, though they are in fact empty—have null extension—have it

[2] Given a chance to add a footnote, I shall mention that Rogers Albritton, Charles Chastain, Keith Donnellan, and Michael Slote (in addition to philosophers mentioned in the text, especially Hilary Putnam), have independently expressed views with points of contact with various aspects of what I say here. Albritton called the problems of necessity and *a prioricity* in natural kinds to my attention, by raising the question whether we could discover that lemons were not fruits. (I am not sure he would accept all my conclusions.) I also recall the influence of early conversations with Albritton and with Peter Geach on the essentiality of origins. The apology in the text still stands; I am aware that the list in this footnote is far from comprehensive. I make no attempt to enumerate those friends and students whose stimulating conversations have helped me. Thomas Nagel and Gilbert Harman deserve special thanks for their help in editing the transcript.

as a matter of contingent fact and not as a matter of any sort of necessity. Well, *that* I don't dispute; but an example which is usually given is the example of *unicorn*. So it is said that though we have all found out that there are no unicorns, of course there *might* have been unicorns. Under certain circumstances there *would* have been unicorns. And this is an example of something I think is not the case. Perhaps according to me the truth should not be put in terms of saying that it is necessary that there should be no unicorns, but just that we can't say under what circumstances there would have been unicorns. Further, I think that even if archeologists or geologists were to discover tomorrow some fossils conclusively showing the existence of animals in the past satisfying everything we know about unicorns from the myth of the unicorn, that would not show that there were unicorns. Now I don't know if I'm going to have a chance to defend this particular view, but it's an example of a surprising one. (I actually gave a seminar in this institution where I talked about this view for a couple of sessions.) So, some of my opinions are somewhat surprising; but let us start out with some area that is perhaps not as surprising and introduce the methodology and problems of these talks.

The first topic in the pair of topics is naming. By a name here I will mean a proper name, i.e., the name of a person, a city, a country, etc. It is well known that modern logicians also are very interested in definite descriptions: phrases of the form 'the $x$ such that $\varphi x$', such as 'the man who corrupted Hadleyburg'. Now, if one and only one man ever corrupted Hadleyburg, then that man is the referent, in the logician's sense, of that description. We will use the term 'name' so that it does *not* include definite descriptions of that sort, but only those things which in ordinary language would be called 'proper names'. If we want a common term to cover names and descriptions, we may use the term 'designator'.

It is a point, made by Donnellan,[3] that under certain circumstances a particular speaker may use a definite description to refer, not to the proper referent, in the sense that I've just defined it, of that description, but to something else which he wants to single out and which he thinks is the proper referent of the description, but which in fact isn't. So you may say, 'The man over there with the champagne in his glass is happy', though he actually only has water in his glass. Now, even though there is no champagne in his glass, and there may be another man in the room who does have champagne in his glass, the speaker *intended* to refer, or maybe, in some sense of 'refer', *did* refer, to the man he thought had the champagne in his glass. Nevertheless, I'm just going to use the term 'referent

[3] Keith Donnellan, 'Reference and Definite Descriptions', *Philosophical Review* 75 (1966), pp. 281–304. See also Leonard Linsky, 'Reference and Referents', in *Philosophy and Ordinary Language* (ed. Caton), University of Illinois Press, Urbana, 1963. Donnellan's distinction seems applicable to names as well as to descriptions. Two men glimpse someone at a distance and think they recognize him as Jones. 'What is Jones doing?' 'Raking the leaves'. If the distant leaf-raker is actually Smith, then in some sense they are *referring* to Smith, even though they both use 'Jones' *as a name of* Jones. In the text, I speak of the 'referent' of a name to mean the thing named by the name—e.g., Jones, not Smith—even though a speaker may sometimes properly be said to use the name to refer to someone else. Perhaps it would have been less misleading to use a technical term, such as 'denote' rather than 'refer'. My use of 'refer' is such as to satisfy the schema, 'The referent of "*X*" is *X*', where '*X*' is replaceable by any name or description. I am tentatively inclined to believe, in opposition to Donnellan, that his remarks about reference have little to do with semantics or truth-conditions, though they may be relevant to a theory of speech-acts. Space limitations do not permit me to explain what I mean by this, much less defend the view, except for a brief remark: Call the referent of a name or description in my sense the 'semantic referent'; for a name, this is the thing named, for a description, the thing uniquely satisfying the description.

Then the speaker may *refer* to something other than the semantic referent if he has appropriate false beliefs. I think this is what happens in the naming (Smith-Jones) cases and also in the Donnellan 'champagne' case; the one requires no theory that names are ambiguous, and the other requires no modification of Russell's theory of descriptions.

of the description' to mean the object uniquely satisfying the conditions in the definite description. This is the sense in which it's been used in the logical tradition. So, if you have a description of the form 'the $x$ such that $\varphi x$', and there is exactly one $x$ such that $\varphi x$, that is the referent of the description.

Now, what is the relation between names and descriptions? There is a well known doctrine of John Stuart Mill, in his book *A System of Logic*, that names have denotation but not connotation. To use one of his examples, when we use the name 'Dartmouth' to describe a certain locality in England, it may be so called because it lies at the mouth of the Dart. But even, he says, had the Dart (that's a river) changed its course so that Dartmouth no longer lay at the mouth of the Dart, we could still with propriety call this place 'Dartmouth', even though the name may suggest that it lies at the mouth of the Dart. Changing Mill's terminology, perhaps we should say that a name such as 'Dartmouth' *does* have a 'connotation' to some people, namely, it *does* connote (not to me—I never thought of this) that any place called 'Dartmouth' lies at the mouth of the Dart. But then in some way it doesn't have a 'sense'. At least, it is not part of the *meaning* of the name 'Dartmouth' that the town so named lies at the mouth of the Dart. Someone who said that Dartmouth did not lie at the Dart's mouth would not contradict himself.

It should not be thought that every phrase of the form 'the $x$ such that $Fx$' is always used in English as a description rather than a name. I guess everyone has heard about The Holy Roman Empire, which was neither holy, Roman nor an empire. Today we have The United Nations. Here it would seem that since these things can be so-called even though they are not Holy Roman United Nations, these phrases should be regarded not as definite descriptions, but as names. In the case of some terms, people might have doubts as to whether they're names or descriptions; like 'God'—does it describe God as the unique divine being or is it a name of God? But such cases needn't necessarily bother us.

Now here I am making a distinction which is certainly made in language. But the classical tradition of modern logic has gone very strongly against Mill's view. Frege and Russell both thought, and seemed to arrive at these conclusions independently of each other, that Mill was wrong in a very strong sense: really a proper name, properly used, simply was a definite description abbreviated or disguised. Frege specifically said that such a description gave the sense of the name.[4]

Now the reasons against Mill's view and in favor of the alternative view adopted by Frege and Russell are really very powerful; and it is hard to see—though one may be suspicious of this view because names don't seem to be disguised descriptions—how the Frege-Russell view, or some suitable variant, can fail to be the case.

Let me give an example of some of the arguments which seem conclusive in favor of the view of Frege and Russell. The basic problem for any view such as Mill's is how we can determine what the referent of a name, as used by a given

[4] Strictly speaking, of course, Russell says that the names don't abbreviate descriptions and don't have any sense; but then he also says that, just because the things that we call 'names' do abbreviate descriptions, they're not really names. So, since 'Walter Scott', according to Russell, does abbreviate a description, 'Walter Scott' is not a name; and the only names that really exist in ordinary language are, perhaps, demonstratives such as 'this' or 'that', used on a particular occasion to refer to an object with which the speaker is 'acquainted' in Russell's sense. Though we won't put things the way Russell does, we could describe Russell as saying that names, as they are ordinarily called, *do* have sense. They have sense in a strong way, namely, we should be able to give a definite description such that the referent of the name, by definition, is the object satisfying the description. Russell himself, since he eliminates descriptions from his primitive notation, seems to hold in 'On Denoting' that the notion of 'sense' is illusory. In reporting Russell's views, we thus deviate from him in two respects. First, we stipulate that 'names' shall be names as ordinarily conceived, not Russell's 'logically proper names'; second, we regard descriptions, and their abbreviations, as having sense.

speaker, is. According to the description view, the answer is clear. If 'Joe Doakes' is just short for 'the man who corrupted Hadleyburg', then whoever corrupted Hadleyburg uniquely is the referent of the name 'Joe Doakes'. However, if there is *not* such a descriptive content to the name, then how do people ever use names to refer to things at all? Well, they may be in a position to point to some things and thus determine the references of certain names ostensively. This was Russell's doctrine of acquaintance, which he thought the so-called genuine or proper names satisfied. But of course ordinary names refer to all sorts of people, like Walter Scott, to whom we can't possibly point. And our reference here seems to be determined by our knowledge of them. Whatever we know about them determines the referent of the name as the unique thing satisfying those properties. For example, if I use the name 'Napoleon', and someone asks, 'To whom are you referring?', I will answer something like, 'Napoleon was emperor of the French in the early part of the nineteenth century; he was eventually defeated at Waterloo', thus giving a uniquely identifying description to determine the referent of the name. Frege and Russell, then, appear to give the natural account of how reference is determined here; Mill appears to give none.

There are subsidiary arguments which, though they are based on more specialized problems, are also motivations for accepting the view. One is that sometimes we may discover that two names have the same referent, and express this by an identity statement. So, for example (I guess this is a hackneyed example), you see a star in the evening and it's called 'Hesperus'. (That's what we call it in the evening, is that right?—I hope it's not the other way around.) We see a star in the morning and call it 'Phosphorus'. Well, then, in fact we find that it's not a star, but is the planet Venus and that Hesperus and Phosphorus are in fact the same. So we express this by 'Hesperus is Phosphorus'. Here we're certainly not just saying of an object that it's identical with itself. This is something that we discovered. A very natural thing to say is that the real content [is that] the star which we saw in the evening is the star which we saw in the morning (or, more accurately, that the thing which we saw in the evening is the thing which we saw in the morning). This, then, gives the real meaning of the identity statement in question; and the analysis in terms of descriptions does this.

Also we may raise the question whether a name has any reference at all when we ask, e.g., whether Aristotle ever existed. It seems natural here to think that what is questioned is not whether this *thing* (man) existed. Once we've *got* the thing, we know that it existed. What really is queried is whether anything answers to the properties we associate with the name—in the case of Aristotle, whether any one Greek philosopher produced certain works, or at least a suitable number of them.

It would be nice to answer all of these arguments. I am not entirely able to see my way clear through every problem of this sort that can be raised. Furthermore, I'm pretty sure that I won't have time to discuss all these questions in these lectures. Nevertheless, I think it's pretty certain that the view of Frege and Russell is false.[5]

[5] When I speak of the Frege-Russell view and its variants, I include only those versions which give a substantive theory of the reference of names. In particular, Quine's proposal that in a 'canonical notation' a name such as 'Socrates' should be replaced by a description 'the Socratizer' (where 'Socratizes' is an invented predicate), and that the description should then be eliminated by Russell's method, was not intended as a theory of reference for names but as a proposed reform of language with certain advantages. The problems discussed here will all apply, *mutatis mutandis*, to the reformed language; in particular, the question, 'How is the reference of "Socrates" determined?' yields to the question, 'How is the extension of "Socratizes" determined?' Of course I do not suggest that Quine has ever claimed the contrary.

Many people have said that the theory of Frege and Russell is false, but, in my opinion, they have abandoned its letter while retaining its spirit, namely, they have used the notion of a cluster concept. Well, what is this? The obvious problem for Frege and Russell, the one which comes immediately to mind, is already mentioned by Frege himself. He said,

> In the case of genuinely proper names like 'Aristotle' opinions as regards their sense may diverge. As such may, e.g., be suggested: Plato's disciple and the teacher of Alexander the Great. Whoever accepts this sense will interpret the meaning of the statement 'Aristotle was born in Stagira', differently from one who interpreted the sense of 'Aristotle' as the Stagirite teacher of Alexander the Great. As long as the nominatum remains the same, these fluctuations in sense are tolerable. But they should be avoided in the system of a demonstrative science and should not appear in a perfect language.[8]

So, according to Frege, there is some sort of looseness or weakness in our language. Some people may give one sense to the name 'Aristotle', others may give another. But of course it is not only that; even a single speaker when asked 'What description are you willing to substitute for the name?' may be quite at a loss. In fact, he may know many things about him; but any particular thing that he knows he may feel clearly expresses a contingent property of the object. If 'Aristotle' meant *the man who taught Alexander the Great*, then saying 'Aristotle was a teacher of Alexander the Great' would be a mere tautology. But surely it isn't; it expresses the fact that Aristotle taught Alexander the Great, something we could discover to be false. So, *being the teacher of Alexander the Great* cannot be part of [the sense of] the name.

[8] Gottlob Frege, 'On Sense and Nominatum', translated by Herbert Feigl in *Readings in Philosophical Analysis* (ed. by Herbert Feigl and Wilfrid Sellars), Appleton Century Crofts, 1949, p. 86.

The most common way out of this difficulty is to say 'really it is not a weakness in ordinary language that we can't substitute a *particular* description for the name; that's all right. What we really associate with the name is a *family* of descriptions.' A good example of this is (if I can find it) in *Philosophical Investigations*, where the idea of family resemblances is introduced and with great power.

Consider this example. If one says 'Moses did not exist', this may mean various things. It may mean: the Israelites did not have a *single* leader when they withdrew from Egypt—or: their leader was not called Moses—or: there cannot have been anyone who accomplished all that the Bible relates of Moses— . . . But when I make a statement about Moses,—am I always ready to substitute some *one* of those descriptions for 'Moses'? I shall perhaps say: by 'Moses' I understand the man who did what the Bible relates of Moses, or at any rate, a good deal of it. But how much? Have I decided how much must be proved false for me to give up my proposition as false? Has the name 'Moses' got a fixed and unequivocal use for me in all possible cases?[7]

According to this view, and a *locus classicus* of it is Searle's article on proper names,[8] the referent of a name is determined not by a single description but by some cluster or family. Whatever in some sense satisfies enough or most of the family is the referent of the name. I shall return to this view later. It may seem, as an analysis of ordinary language, quite a bit more plausible than that of Frege and Russell. It may seem to keep all the virtues and remove the defects of this theory.

Let me say (and this will introduce us to another new topic before I really consider this theory of naming) that there are two ways in which the cluster concept theory, or even the

[7] Ludwig Wittgenstein, *Philosophical Investigations*, translated by G. E. M. Anscombe, MacMillan, 1953, § 79.

[8] John R. Searle, 'Proper Names', *Mind* 67 (1958), 166–73.

theory which requires a single description, can be viewed. One way of regarding it says that the cluster or the single description actually gives the meaning of the name; and when someone says 'Walter Scott', he means *the man such that such and such and such and such*.

Now another view might be that even though the description in some sense doesn't give the *meaning* of the name, it is what *determines its reference* and although the phrase 'Walter Scott' isn't *synonymous* with 'the man such that such and such and such and such', or even maybe with the family (if something can be synonymous with a family), the family or the single description is what is used to determine to whom someone is referring when he says 'Walter Scott'. Of course, if when we hear his beliefs about Walter Scott we find that they are actually much more nearly true of Salvador Dali, then according to this theory the reference of this name is going to be Mr. Dali, not Scott. There are writers, I think, who explicitly deny that names have meaning at all even more strongly than I would but still use this picture of how the referent of the name gets determined. A good case in point is Paul Ziff, who says, very emphatically, that names don't have meaning at all, [that] they are not a part of language in some sense. But still, when he talks about how we determine what the reference of the name was, then he gives this picture. Unfortunately I don't have the passage in question with me, but this is what he says.[9]

[9] Ziff's most detailed statement of his version of the cluster-of-descriptions theory of the reference of names is in 'About God', reprinted in *Philosophical Turnings*, Cornell University Press, Ithaca, and Oxford University Press, London, 1966, pp. 94–96. A briefer statement is in his *Semantic Analysis*, Cornell University Press, Ithaca, 1960, pp. 102–05 (esp. pp. 103–04). The latter passage suggests that names of things with which we are acquainted should be treated somewhat differently (using ostension and baptism) from names of historical figures, where the reference is determined by (a cluster of) associated descriptions. On p. 93 of *Semantic Analysis* Ziff states that 'simple

The difference between using this theory as a theory of meaning and using it as a theory of reference will come out a little more clearly later on. But some of the attractiveness of the theory is lost if it isn't supposed to give the meaning of the name; for some of the solutions of problems that I've just mentioned will not be right, or at least won't clearly be right, if the description doesn't give the meaning of the name. For example, if someone said 'Aristotle does not exist' *means* 'there is no man doing such and such', or in the example from Wittgenstein, 'Moses does not exist', *means* 'no man did such and such', that might depend (and in fact, I think, does depend) on taking the theory in question as a theory of the meaning of the name 'Moses', not just as a theory of its reference. Well, I don't know. Perhaps all that is immediate now is the other way around: if 'Moses' means the same as 'the man who did such and such' then to say that Moses did not exist is to say that the man who did such and such did not exist, that is, that no one person did such and such. If, on the other hand, 'Moses' is not synonymous with any description, then even if its reference is in some sense determined by a description, statements containing the name cannot in general be *analyzed* by replacing the name by a description, though they may be materially equivalent to statements containing a description. So the analysis of singular existence statements mentioned above will have to be given up, unless it is established by some special argument, independent of a general theory of the meaning of names; and the same applies to identity statements. In any case, I think it's false that 'Moses exists' means that at all.

---

strong generalization(s) about proper names' are impossible; 'one can only say what is so for the most part ...' Nevertheless Ziff clearly states that a cluster-of-descriptions theory is a reasonable such rough statement, at least for historical figures. For Ziff's view that proper names ordinarily are not words of the language and ordinarily do not have meaning, see pp. 85–89 and 93–94 of *Semantic Analysis*.

So we won't have to see if such a special argument can be drawn up.[10]

Before I go any further into this problem, I want to talk about another distinction which will be important in the methodology of these talks. Philosophers have talked (and, of course, there has been considerable controversy in recent years over the meaningfulness of these notions) [about] various categories of truth, which are called '*a priori*', 'analytic', 'necessary'—and sometimes even 'certain' is thrown into this batch. The terms are often used as if *whether* there are things answering to these concepts is an interesting question, but we might as well regard them all as meaning the same thing. Now, everyone remembers Kant (a bit) as making a distinction between '*a priori*' and 'analytic'. So maybe this distinction is still made. In contemporary discussion very few people, if any, distinguish between the concepts of statements being *a priori* and their being necessary. At any rate I shall *not* use the terms '*a priori*' and 'necessary' interchangeably here.

Consider what the traditional characterizations of such terms as '*a priori*' and 'necessary' are. First the notion of a prioricity is a concept of epistemology. I guess the traditional characterization from Kant goes something like: *a priori* truths are those which can be known independently of any experience. This introduces another problem before we get off the ground, because there's another modality in the characterization of '*a priori*', namely, it is supposed to be something which *can* be known independently of any experience. That means that in some sense it's *possible* (whether we do or do not in fact know it independently of any experience) to know this independently of any experience. And possible for whom? For God? For the Martians?

[10] Those determinists who deny the importance of the individual in history may well argue that had Moses never existed, someone else would have arisen to achieve all that he did. Their claim cannot be refuted by appealing to a correct philosophical theory of the meaning of 'Moses exists'.

Or just for people with minds like ours? To make this all clear might [involve] a host of problems all of its own about what sort of possibility is in question here. It might be best therefore, instead of using the phrase '*a priori* truth', to the extent that one uses it at all, to stick to the question of whether a particular person or knower knows something *a priori* or believes it true on the basis of *a priori* evidence.

I won't go further too much into the problems that might arise with the notion of a prioricity here. I will say that some philosophers somehow change the modality in this characterization from *can* to *must*. They think that if something belongs to the realm of *a priori* knowledge, it couldn't possibly be known empirically. This is just a mistake. Something may belong in the realm of such statements that *can* be known *a priori* but still may be known by particular people on the basis of experience. To give a really common sense example: anyone who has worked with a computing machine knows that the computing machine may give an answer to whether such and such a number is prime. No one has calculated or proved that the number is prime; but the machine has given the answer: this number is prime. We, then, if we believe that the number is prime, believe it on the basis of our knowledge of the laws of physics, the construction of the machine, and so on. We therefore do not believe this on the basis of purely *a priori* evidence. We believe it (if anything is *a posteriori* at all) on the basis of *a posteriori* evidence. Nevertheless, maybe this could be known *a priori* by someone who made the requisite calculations. So '*can* be known *a priori*' doesn't mean '*must* be known *a priori*'.

The second concept which is in question is that of necessity. Sometimes this is used in an epistemological way and might then just mean *a priori*. And of course, sometimes it is used in a physical way when people distinguish between physical and logical necessity. But what I am concerned with here is a notion which is not a notion of epistemology but of metaphysics, in some (I hope) nonpejorative sense. We ask whether something might have been true, or might have been false. Well, if something is false, it's obviously not necessarily true. If it is true, might it have been otherwise? Is it possible that, in this respect, the world should have been different from the way it is? If the answer is 'no', then this fact about the world is a necessary one. If the answer is 'yes', then this fact about the world is a contingent one. This in and of itself has nothing to do with anyone's knowledge of anything. It's certainly a philosophical thesis, and not a matter of obvious definitional equivalence, either that everything *a priori* is necessary or that everything necessary is *a priori*. Both concepts may be vague. That may be another problem. But at any rate they are dealing with two different domains, two different areas, the epistemological and the metaphysical. Consider, say, Fermat's last theorem—or the Goldbach conjecture. The Goldbach conjecture says that an even number greater than 2 must be the sum of two prime numbers. If this is true, it is presumably necessary, and, if it is false, presumably necessarily false. We are taking the classical view of mathematics here and assume that in mathematical reality it is either true or false.

If the Goldbach conjecture is false, then there is an even number, $n$, greater than 2, such that for no primes $p_1$ and $p_2$, both $< n$, does $n = p_1 + p_2$. This fact about $n$, if true, is verifiable by direct computation, and thus is necessary if the results of arithmetical computations are necessary. On the other hand, if the conjecture is true, then every even number exceeding 2 is the sum of two primes. Could it then be the case that, although in fact every such even number is the sum of two primes, there might have been such an even number which was not the sum of two primes? What would that mean? Such a number would have to be one of 4, 6, 8, 10, . . .; and, by hypothesis, since we are assuming Goldbach's conjecture to be true, each of these can be shown, again by direct computation, to be the sum of two primes. Goldbach's conjecture, then, cannot be contingently true or false; whatever truth-value it has belongs to it by necessity.

But what we can say, of course, is that right now, as far as we know, the question can come out either way. So, in the absence of a mathematical proof deciding this question, none of us has any *a priori* knowledge about this question in either direction. We don't know whether Goldbach's conjecture is true or false. So right now we certainly don't know anything *a priori* about it.

Perhaps it will be alleged that we *can* in principle know *a priori* whether it is true. Well, maybe we can. Of course an infinite mind which can search through all the numbers can or could. But I don't know whether a finite mind can or could. Maybe there just is no mathematical proof whatsoever which decides the conjecture. At any rate this might or might not be the case. Maybe there is a mathematical proof deciding this question; maybe every mathematical question is decidable by an intuitive proof or disproof. Hilbert thought so; others have thought not; still others have thought the question unintelligible unless the notion of intuitive proof is replaced by that of formal proof in a single system. Certainly no one formal system decides all mathematical questions, as we know from Gödel. At any rate, and this is the important thing, the question is not trivial; even though someone said that it's necessary, if true at all, that every even number is the sum of two primes, it doesn't follow that anyone knows anything *a priori* about it. It doesn't even seem to me to follow without some further philosophical argument (it is an interesting philosophical question) that anyone *could* know anything *a priori* about it. The 'could', as I said, involves some other modality. We mean that even if no one, perhaps even in the future, knows or will know *a priori* whether Goldbach's conjecture is right, in principle there is a way, which *could* have been used, of answering the question *a priori*. This assertion is not trivial.

The terms 'necessary' and '*a priori*', then, as applied to statements, are *not* obvious synonyms. There may be a philosophical argument connecting them, perhaps even identifying them; but an argument is required, not simply the observation that the two terms are clearly interchangeable. (I will argue below that in fact they are not even coextensive—that necessary *a posteriori* truths, and probably contingent *a priori* truths, both exist.)

I think people have thought that these two things must mean the same for these reasons:

First, if something not only happens to be true in the actual world but is also true in all possible worlds, then, of course, just by running through all the possible worlds in our heads, we ought to be able with enough effort to see, if a statement is necessary, that it is necessary, and thus know it *a priori*. But really this is not so obviously feasible at all.

Second, I guess it's thought that, conversely, if something is known *a priori* it must be necessary, because it was known without looking at the world. If it depended on some contingent feature of the actual world, how could you know it without looking? Maybe the actual world is one of the possible worlds in which it would have been false. This depends on the thesis that there can't be a way of knowing about the actual world without looking that wouldn't be a way of knowing the same thing about every possible world. This involves problems of epistemology and the nature of knowledge; and of course it is very vague as stated. But it is not really *trivial* either. More important than any particular example of something which is alleged to be necessary and not *a priori* or *a priori* and not necessary, is to see that the notions are different, that it's not trivial to argue on the basis of something's being something which maybe we can only know *a posteriori*, that it's not a necessary truth. It's not trivial, just because something is known in some sense *a priori*, that what is known is a necessary truth.

Another term used in philosophy is 'analytic'. Here it won't be too important to get any clearer about this in this talk. The common examples of analytic statements, nowadays, are like 'bachelors are unmarried'. Kant (someone just pointed out to me) gives as an example 'gold is a yellow metal', which seems to me an extraordinary one, because it's something I think that can turn out to be false. At any rate, let's just make it a matter of stipulation that an analytic statement is, in some sense, true by virtue of its meaning and true in all possible worlds by virtue of its meaning. Then something which is analytically true will be both necessary and *a priori*. (That's sort of stipulative.)

Another category I mentioned was that of certainty. Whatever certainty is, it's clearly not obviously the case that everything which is necessary is certain. Certainty is another epistemological notion. Something can be known, or at least rationally believed, *a priori*, without being quite certain. You've read a proof in the math book; and, though you think it's correct, maybe you've made a mistake. You often do make mistakes of this kind. You've made a computation, perhaps with an error.

There is one more question I want to go into in a preliminary way. Some philosophers have distinguished between essentialism, the belief in modality *de re*, and a mere advocacy of necessity, the belief in modality *de dicto*. Now, some people say: Let's *give* you the concept of necessity.[11] A much worse

[11] By the way, it's a common attitude in philosophy to think that one shouldn't introduce a notion until it's been rigorously defined (according to some popular notion of rigor). Here I am just dealing with an intuitive notion and will keep on the level of an intuitive notion. That is, we think that some things, though they are in fact the case, might have been otherwise. I might not have given these lectures today. If that's right, then it is *possible* that I

thing, something creating great additional problems, is whether we can say of any particular that it has necessary or contingent properties, even make the distinction between necessary and contingent properties. Look, it's only a *statement* or a *state of affairs* that can be either necessary or contingent! Whether a *particular* necessarily or contingently has a certain property depends on the way it's described. This is perhaps closely related to the view that the way we refer to particular things is by a description. What is Quine's famous example? If we consider the number 9, does it have the property of necessary oddness? Has that number got to be odd in all possible worlds? Certainly it's true in all possible worlds, let's say, it couldn't have been otherwise, that *nine* is odd. Of course, 9 could also be equally well picked out as *the number of planets*. It is *not* necessary, not true in all possible worlds, that the number of planets is odd. For example if there had been eight planets, the number of planets would not have been odd. And so it's thought: Was it necessary or contingent that Nixon won the election? (It might seem contingent, unless one has some view of some inexorable processes. . . .) But this is a contingent property of Nixon only relative to our referring to him as 'Nixon' (assuming 'Nixon' doesn't mean 'the man who won the election at such and such a time'). But if we designate Nixon as 'the man who won the election in 1968', then it will be a necessary truth, of course, that the man who won the election in 1968, won the election in 1968. Similarly, whether an object has the same property in all possible worlds depends

---

wouldn't have given these lectures today. Quite a different question is the epistemological question, how any particular person knows that I gave these lectures today. I suppose in that case he does know this is *a posteriori*. But, if someone were born with an innate belief that I was going to give these lectures today, who knows? Right now, anyway, let's suppose that people know this *a posteriori*. At any rate, the two questions being asked are different.

not just on the object itself, but on how it is described. So it's argued.

It is even suggested in the literature, that though a notion of necessity may have some sort of intuition behind it (we do think some things could have been otherwise; other things we don't think could have been otherwise), this notion [of a distinction between necessary and contingent properties] is just a doctrine made up by some bad philosopher, who (I guess) didn't realize that there are several ways of referring to the same thing. I don't know if some philosophers have not realized this; but at any rate it is very far from being true that this idea [that a property can meaningfully be held to be essential or accidental to an object independently of its description] is a notion which has no intuitive content, which means nothing to the ordinary man. Suppose that someone said, pointing to Nixon, 'That's the guy who might have lost'. Someone else says 'Oh no, if you describe him as "Nixon", then he might have lost; but, of course, describing him as the winner, then it is not true that he might have lost'. Now which one is being the philosopher, here, the unintuitive man? It seems to me obviously to be the second. The second man has a philosophical theory. The first man would say, and with great conviction, 'Well, of course, the winner of the election *might have been someone else*. The actual winner, had the course of the campaign been different, might have been the loser, and someone else the winner; or there might have been no election at all. So, such terms as "the winner" and "the loser" don't designate the same objects in all possible worlds. On the other hand, the term "Nixon" is just a *name* of *this man*'. When you ask whether it is necessary or contingent that *Nixon* won the election, you are asking the intuitive question whether in some counterfactual situation, *this man* would in fact have lost the election. If someone thinks that the notion of a necessary or contingent property (forget whether there *are* any nontrivial necessary properties [and consider] just the *meaningfulness* of the notion[12]) is a philosopher's notion with no intuitive content, he is wrong. Of course, some philosophers think that something's having intuitive content is very inconclusive evidence in favor of it. I think it is very heavy evidence in favor of anything, myself. I really don't know, in a way, what more conclusive evidence one can have about anything, ultimately speaking. But, in any event, people who think the notion of accidental property unintuitive have intuition reversed, I think.

Why have they thought this? While there are many motivations for people thinking this, one is this: The question of essential properties so-called is supposed to be equivalent (and it is equivalent) to the question of 'identity across possible worlds'. Suppose we have someone, Nixon, and there's another possible world where there is no one with all the properties Nixon has in the actual world. Which one of these other people, if any, is Nixon? Surely you must give some criterion of identity here! If you have a criterion of identity, then you just look in the other possible worlds at the man who is Nixon; and the question whether, in that other possible world, Nixon has certain properties, is well defined. It is also supposed to be well defined, in terms of such notions, whether it's true in all possible worlds, or there are some possible worlds in which Nixon didn't win the election. But, it's said, the problems of giving such criteria of identity are very difficult. Sometimes

[12] The example I gave asserts a certain property—electoral victory—to be *accidental* to Nixon, independently of how he is described. Of course, if the notion of accidental property is meaningful, the notion of essential property must be meaningful also. This is not to say that there *are* any essential properties—though, in fact, I think there are. The usual argument questions the *meaningfulness* of essentialism, and says that whether a property is accidental or essential to an object depends on how it is described. It is thus *not* the view that all properties are accidental. Of course, it is also not the view, held by some idealists, that all properties are essential, all relations internal.

in the case of numbers it might seem easier (but even here it's argued that it's quite arbitrary). For example, one might say, and this is surely the truth, that if position in the series of numbers is what makes the number 9 what it is, then if (in another world) the number of planets had been 8, the number of planets would be a different number from the one it actually is. You wouldn't say that that number then is to be identified with our number 9 in this world. In the case of other types of objects, say people, material objects, things like that, has anyone given a set of necessary and sufficient conditions for identity across possible worlds?

Really, adequate necessary and sufficient conditions for identity which do not beg the question are very rare in any case. Mathematics is the only case I really know of where they are given even *within* a possible world, to tell the truth. I don't know of such conditions for identity of material objects over time, or for people. Everyone knows what a problem this is. But, let's forget about that. What seems to be more objectionable is that this depends on the wrong way of looking at what a possible world is. One thinks, in this picture, of a possible world as if it were like a foreign country. One looks upon it as an observer. Maybe Nixon has moved to the other country and maybe he hasn't, but one is given only qualities. One can observe all his qualities, but, of course, one doesn't observe that someone is Nixon. One observes that something has red hair (or green or yellow) but not whether something is Nixon. So we had better have a way of telling in terms of properties when we run into the same thing as we saw before; we had better have a way of telling, when we come across one of these other possible worlds, who was Nixon.

Some logicians in their formal treatment of modal logic may encourage this picture. A prominent example, perhaps, is myself. Nevertheless, intuitively speaking, it seems to me not to be the right way of thinking about the possible worlds. A possible world isn't a distant country that we are coming across, or viewing through a telescope. Generally speaking, another possible world is too far away. Even if we travel faster than light, we won't get to it. A possible world is *given by the descriptive conditions we associate with it.* What do we mean when we say 'In some other possible world I would not have given this lecture today?' We just imagine the situation where I didn't decide to give this lecture or decided to give it on some other day. Of course, we don't imagine everything that is true or false, but only those things relevant to my giving the lecture; but, in theory, everything needs to be decided to make a total description of the world. We can't really imagine that except in part; that, then, is a 'possible world'. Why can't it be part of the *description* of a possible world that it contains *Nixon* and that in that world *Nixon* didn't win the election? It might be a question, of course, whether such a world *is* possible. (Here it would seem, *prima facie*, to be clearly possible.) But, once we see that such a situation is possible, then we are given that the man who might have lost the election or did lose the election in this possible world is Nixon, because that's part of the description of the world. 'Possible worlds' are *stipulated*, not *discovered* by powerful telescopes. There is no reason why we cannot *stipulate* that, in talking about what would have happened to Nixon in a certain counterfactual situation, we are talking about what would have happened to *him*.

Of course, if someone makes the demand that every possible world has to be described in a purely qualitative way, we can't say, 'Suppose Nixon had lost the election', we must say, instead, something like, 'Suppose a man with a dog named Checkers, who looks like a certain David Frye impersonation, is in a certain possible world and loses the election.' Well, does he resemble Nixon enough to be identified with Nixon? A very explicit and blatant example of this way of looking at things is David Lewis's counterpart theory,[13] but the literature on quantified modality is replete with it.[14] Why need we make this demand? That is not the way we ordinarily think of counterfactual situations. We just say 'suppose this man had

[13] David K. Lewis, 'Counterpart Theory and Quantified Modal Logic', *Journal of Philosophy* **65** (1968), 113–126. Lewis's elegant paper also suffers from a purely formal difficulty: on his interpretation of quantified modality, the familiar law $(y)((x)A(x) \supset A(y))$ fails, if $A(x)$ is allowed to contain modal operators. (For example, $(\exists y)((x) \Diamond (x \neq y))$ is satisfiable but $(\exists y) \Diamond (y \neq y)$ is not.) Since Lewis's formal model follows rather naturally from his philosophical views on counterparts, and since the failure of universal instantiation for modal properties is intuitively bizarre, it seems to me that this failure constitutes an additional argument against the plausibility of his philosophical views. There are other, lesser, formal difficulties as well. I cannot elaborate here.

Strictly speaking, Lewis's view is not a view of 'transworld identification'. Rather, he thinks that similarities across possible worlds determine a counter-part relation which need be neither symmetric nor transitive. The counterpart of something in another possible world is *never* identical with the thing itself. Thus if we say 'Humphrey might have won the election (if only he had done such-and-such), we are not talking about something that might have happened to *Humphrey* but to someone else, a "counterpart".' Probably, however, Humphrey could not care less whether someone *else*, no matter how much resembling him, would have been victorious in another possible world. Thus, Lewis's view seems to me even more bizarre than the usual notions of trans-world identification that it replaces. The important issues, however, are common to the two views: the supposition that other possible worlds are like other dimensions of a more inclusive universe, that they can be given only by purely qualitative descriptions, and that therefore either the identity relation or the counterpart relation must be established in terms of qualitative resemblance.

Many have pointed out to me that the father of counterpart theory is probably Leibnitz. I will not go into such a historical question here. It would also be interesting to compare Lewis's views with the Wheeler-Everett interpretation of quantum mechanics. I suspect that this view of physics may suffer from philosophical problems analogous to Lewis's counterpart theory; it is certainly very similar in spirit.

[14] Another *locus classicus* of the views I am criticizing, with more philosophical exposition than Lewis's paper, is a paper by David Kaplan on trans-world identification. Unfortunately, this paper has never been published. It does not represent Kaplan's present position.

lost'. It is *given* that the possible world contains *this man*, and that in that world, he had lost. There may be a problem about what intuitions about possibility come to. But, if we have such an intuition about the possibility of *that* (*this man's* electoral loss), then it is about the possibility of *that*. It need not be identified with the possibility of a man looking like such and such, or holding such and such political views, or otherwise qualitatively described, having lost. We can point to the *man*, and ask what might have happened to *him*, had events been different.

It might be said 'Let's suppose that this is true. It comes down to the same thing, because whether Nixon could have had certain properties, different from the ones he actually has, is equivalent to the question whether the criteria of identity across possible worlds include that Nixon does not have these properties'. But it doesn't really come to the same thing, because the usual notion of a criterion of transworld identity demands that we give purely qualitative necessary and sufficient conditions for someone being Nixon. If we can't imagine a possible world in which Nixon doesn't have a certain property, then it's a necessary condition of someone being Nixon. Or a necessary property of Nixon that he [has] that property. For example, supposing Nixon is in fact a human being, it would seem that we cannot think of a possible counterfactual situation in which he was, say, an inanimate object; perhaps it is not even possible for him not to have been a human being. Then it will be a necessary fact about Nixon that in all possible worlds where he exists at all, he is human or anyway he is not an inanimate object. This has nothing to do with any requirement that there be purely qualitative *sufficient* conditions for Nixonhood which we can spell out. And should there be? Maybe there is some argument that there should be, but we can consider these questions about *necessary* conditions without going into any question about *sufficient* conditions.

Further, even if there were a purely qualitative set of necessary and sufficient conditions for being Nixon, the view I advocate would not demand that we find these conditions *before* we can ask whether Nixon might have won the election, nor does it demand that we restate the question in terms of such conditions. We can simply consider *Nixon* and ask what might have happened to *him* had various circumstances been different. So the two views, the two ways of looking at things, do seem to me to make a difference.

Notice this question, whether Nixon could not have been a human being, is a clear case where the question asked is not epistemological. Suppose Nixon actually turned out to be an automaton. That might happen. We might need evidence whether Nixon is a human being or an automaton. But that is a question about our knowledge. The question of whether Nixon might have not been a human being, given that he is one, is not a question about knowledge, *a posteriori* or *a priori*. It's a question about, even though such and such things are the case, what might have been the case otherwise.

This table is composed of molecules. Might it not have been composed of molecules? Certainly it was a scientific discovery of great moment that it was composed of molecules (or atoms). But could anything be this very object and not be composed of molecules? Certainly there is some feeling that the answer to that must be 'no'. At any rate, it's hard to imagine under what circumstances you would have this very object and find that it is not composed of molecules. A quite different question is whether it is in fact composed of molecules in the actual world and how we know this. (I will go into more detail about these questions about essence later on.)

I wish at this point to introduce something which I need in the methodology of discussing the theory of names that I'm talking about. We need the notion of 'identity across possible worlds' as it's usually and, as I think, somewhat misleadingly called,[15] to explicate one distinction that I want to make now. What's the difference between asking whether it's necessary that 9 is greater than 7 or whether it's necessary that the number of planets is greater than 7? Why does one show anything more about essence than the other? The answer to this might be intuitively 'Well, look, the number of planets might have been different from what it in fact is. It doesn't make any sense, though, to say that nine might have been different from what it in fact is'. Let's use some terms quasi-technically. Let's call something a *rigid designator* if in every possible world it designates the same object, a *nonrigid* or *accidental designator* if that is not the case. Of course we don't require that the objects exist in all possible worlds. Certainly Nixon might not have existed if his parents had not gotten married, in the normal course of things. When we think of a property as essential to an object we usually mean that it is true of that object in any case where it would have existed. A rigid designator of a necessary existent can be called *strongly rigid*.

One of the intuitive theses I will maintain in these talks is that *names* are rigid designators. Certainly they seem to satisfy the intuitive test mentioned above: although someone other than the U.S. President in 1970 might have been the U.S. President in 1970 (e.g., Humphrey might have), no one other than Nixon might have been Nixon. In the same way, a

[15] Misleadingly, because the phrase suggests that there is a special problem of 'transworld identification', that we cannot trivially stipulate whom or what we are talking about when we imagine another possible world. The term 'possible world' may also mislead; perhaps it suggests the 'foreign country' picture. I have sometimes used 'counterfactual situation' in the text; Michael Slote has suggested that 'possible state (or history) of the world' might be less misleading than 'possible world'. It is better still, to avoid confusion, not to say, 'In some possible world, Humphrey would have won' but rather, simply, 'Humphrey might have won'. The apparatus of possible words has (I hope) been very useful as far as the set-theoretic model-theory of quantified modal logic is concerned, but has encouraged philosophical pseudo-problems and misleading pictures.

designator rigidly designates a certain object if it designates that object wherever the object exists; if, in addition, the object is a necessary existent, the designator can be called *strongly rigid*. For example, 'the President of the U.S. in 1970' designates a certain man, Nixon; but someone else (e.g., Humphrey) might have been the President in 1970, and Nixon might not have; so this designator is not rigid.

In these lectures, I will argue, intuitively, that proper names are rigid designators, for although the man (Nixon) might not have been the President, it is not the case that he might not have been Nixon (though he might not have been *called* 'Nixon'). Those who have argued that to make sense of the notion of rigid designator, we must antecedently make sense of 'criteria of transworld identity' have precisely reversed the cart and the horse; it is *because* we can refer (rigidly) to Nixon, and stipulate that we are speaking of what might have happened to *him* (under certain circumstances), that 'transworld identifications' are unproblematic in such cases.[16]

The tendency to demand purely qualitative descriptions of counterfactual situations has many sources. One, perhaps, is the confusion of the epistemological and the metaphysical, between a prioricity and necessity. If someone identifies necessity with a prioricity, and thinks that objects are named by means of uniquely identifying properties, he may think that it is the properties used to identify the object which, being known about it *a priori*, must be used to identify it in all possible worlds, to find out which object is Nixon. As against this, I repeat: (1) Generally, things aren't 'found out' about a counterfactual situation, they are stipulated; (2) possible worlds

[16] Of course I don't imply that language contains a name for every object. Demonstratives can be used as rigid designators, and free variables can be used as rigid designators of unspecified objects. Of course when we specify a counterfactual situation, we do not describe the whole possible world, but only the portion which interests us.

need not be given purely qualitatively, as if we were looking at them through a telescope. And we will see shortly that the properties an object has in every counterfactual world have nothing to do with properties used to identify it in the actual world.[17]

Does the 'problem' of 'transworld identification' make any sense? Is it *simply* a pseudo-problem? The following, it seems to me, can be said for it. Although the statement that England fought Germany in 1943 perhaps cannot be *reduced* to any statement about individuals, nevertheless in some sense it is not a fact 'over and above' the collection of all facts about persons, and their behavior over history. The sense in which facts about nations are not facts 'over and above' those about persons can be expressed in the observation that a description of the world mentioning all facts about persons but omitting those about nations can be a *complete* description of the world, from which the facts about nations follow. Similarly, perhaps, facts about material objects are not facts 'over and above' facts about their constituent molecules. We may then ask, given a description of a non-actualized possible situation in terms of people, whether England still exists in that situation, or whether a certain nation (described, say, as the one where Jones lives) which would exist in that situation, is England. Similarly, given certain counterfactual vicissitudes in the history of the molecules of a table, *T*, one may ask whether *T* would exist, in that situation, or whether a certain bunch of molecules, which in that situation would constitute a table, constitute the very same table *T*. In each case, we seek criteria of identity across possible worlds for certain particulars in terms of those for other, more 'basic', particulars. If statements about nations (or tribes) are not *reducible* to those about other more 'basic' constituents, if there is some 'open texture' in the relationship between them, we can hardly expect to give hard and fast identity criteria;

[17] See Lecture I, p. 53 (on Nixon), and Lecture II, pp. 74–7.

nevertheless, in concrete cases we may be able to answer whether a certain bunch of molecules would still constitute $T$, though in some cases the answer may be indeterminate. I think similar remarks apply to the problem of identity over time; here too we are usually concerned with determinacy, the identity of a 'complex' particular in terms of more 'basic' ones. (For example, if various parts of a table are replaced, is it the same object?[18])

Such a conception of 'transworld identification', however, differs considerably from the usual one. First, although we can try to describe the world in terms of molecules, there is no impropriety in describing it in terms of grosser entities: the statement that *this table* might have been placed in another room is perfectly proper, in and of itself. We *need* not use the description in terms of molecules, or even grosser parts of the table, though we *may*. Unless we assume that some particulars are 'ultimate', 'basic' particulars, no type of description need be regarded as privileged. We can ask whether *Nixon* might have lost the election without further subtlety, and usually no further subtlety is required. Second, it is not assumed that necessary and sufficient conditions for what kinds of collections

[18] There is some vagueness here. If a chip, or molecule, of a given table had been replaced by another one, we would be content to say that we have the same table. But if too many chips were different, we would seem to have a different one. The same problem can, of course, arise for identity over time.

Where the identity relation is vague, it may seem intransitive; a chain of apparent identities may yield an apparent non-identity. Some sort of 'counterpart' notion (though not with Lewis's philosophical underpinnings of resemblance, foreign country worlds, etc.), may have some utility here. One could say that strict identity applies only to the particulars (the molecules), and the counterpart relation to the particulars 'composed' of them, the tables. The counterpart relation can then be declared to be vague and intransitive. It seems, however, utopian to suppose that we will ever reach a level of ultimate, basic particulars for which identity relations are never vague and the danger of intransitivity is eliminated. The danger usually does not arise in practice, so we ordinarily can speak simply of identity without worry. Logicians have not developed a logic of vagueness.

of molecules make up this table are possible; this fact I just mentioned. Third, the attempted notion deals with criteria of identity of particulars in terms of other *particulars*, not qualities. I can refer to the table before me, and ask what might have happened to it under certain circumstances; I can also refer to its molecules. If, on the other hand, it is demanded that I describe each counterfactual situation purely qualitatively, then I can only ask whether *a table*, of such and such color, and so on, would have certain properties; whether the table in question would be *this table*, table *T*, is indeed moot, since all reference to objects, as opposed to qualities, has disappeared. It is often said that, if a counterfactual situation is described as one which would have happened to *Nixon*, and if it is not assumed that such a description is reducible to a purely qualitative one, then mysterious 'bare particulars' are assumed, propertyless substrata underlying the qualities. This is not so: I think that Nixon is a Republican, not merely that he lies in back of Republicanism, whatever that means; I also think he might have been a Democrat. The same holds for any other properties Nixon may possess, except that some of these properties may be essential. What I do deny is that a particular is nothing but a 'bundle of qualities', whatever that may mean. If a quality is an abstract object, a bundle of qualities is an object of an even higher degree of abstraction, not a particular. Philosophers have come to the opposite view through a false dilemma: they have asked, are these objects *behind* the bundle of qualities, or is the object *nothing but* the bundle? Neither is the case; this table is wooden, brown, in the room, etc. It has all these properties and is not a thing without properties, behind them; but it should not therefore be identified with the set, or 'bundle', of its properties, nor with the subset of its essential properties. Don't ask: how can I identify this table in another possible world, except by its properties? I have the table in my hands, I can point to it, and when I ask whether *it* might have been in another room, I am talking, by definition, about *it*. I don't have to identify it after seeing it through a telescope. If I am talking about it, I am talking about *it*, in the same way as when I say that our hands might have been painted green, I have stipulated that I am talking about greenness. Some properties of an object may be essential to it, in that it could not have failed to have them. But these properties are not used to identify the object in another possible world, for such an identification is not needed. Nor need the essential properties of an object be the properties used to identify it in the actual world, if indeed it is identified in the actual world by means of properties (I have up to now left the question open).

So: the question of transworld identification makes *some* sense, in terms of asking about the identity of an object *via* questions about its component parts. But these parts are not qualities, and it is not an object resembling the given one which is in question. Theorists have often said that we identify objects across possible worlds as objects resembling the given one in the most important respects. On the contrary, Nixon, had he decided to act otherwise, might have avoided politics like the plague, though privately harboring radical opinions. Most important, even when we *can* replace questions about an object by questions about its parts, we *need* not do so. We can refer to the object and ask what might have happened to *it*. So, we do not begin with worlds (which are supposed somehow to be real, and whose qualities, but not whose objects, are perceptible to us), and then ask about criteria of transworld identification; on the contrary, we begin with the objects, which we *have*, and can identify, in the actual world. We can then ask whether certain things might have been true of the objects.

Above I said that the Frege-Russell view that names are introduced by description could be taken either as a theory of the meaning of names (Frege and Russell seemed to take it this way) or merely as a theory of their reference. Let me give an example, not involving what would usually be called a 'proper name,' to illustrate this. Suppose someone stipulates that 100 degrees centigrade is to be the temperature at which water boils at sea level. This isn't completely precise because the pressure may vary at sea level. Of course, historically, a more precise definition was given later. But let's suppose that this were the definition. Another sort of example in the literature is that one meter is to be the length of *S* where *S* is a certain stick or bar in Paris. (Usually people who like to talk about these definitions then try to make 'the length of' into an 'operational' concept. But it's not important.)

Wittgenstein says something very puzzling about this. He says: 'There is one thing of which one can say neither that it is one meter long nor that it is not one meter long, and that is the standard meter in Paris. But this is, of course, not to ascribe any extraordinary property to it, but only to mark its peculiar role in the language game of measuring with a meter rule.'[19] This seems to be a very 'extraordinary property', actually, for any stick to have. I think he must be wrong. If the stick is a stick, for example, 39·37 inches long (I assume we have some different standard for inches), why isn't it one meter long? Anyway, let's suppose that he is wrong and that the stick is one meter long. Part of the problem which is bothering Wittgenstein is, of course, that this stick serves as a standard of length and so we can't attribute length to it. Be this as it may (well, it may not be), is the statement 'stick *S* is one meter long', a necessary truth? Of course its length might vary in time. We could make the definition more precise by stipulating that one meter is to be the length of *S* at a fixed time $t_0$. Is it then a necessary truth that stick *S* is one meter long at time $t_0$? Someone who thinks that everything one knows *a priori* is necessary might think: 'This is the *definition* of a meter. By

[19] *Philosophical Investigations*, § 50.

definition, stick $S$ is one meter long at $t_0$. That's a necessary truth.' But there seems to me to be no reason so to conclude, even for a man who uses the stated definition of 'one meter'. For he's using this definition not to *give the meaning* of what he called the 'meter', but to *fix the reference*. (For such an abstract thing as a unit of length, the notion of reference may be unclear. But let's suppose it's clear enough for the present purposes.) He uses it to fix a reference. There is a certain length which he wants to mark out. He marks it out by an accidental property, namely that there is a stick of that length. Someone else might mark out the same reference by another accidental property. But in any case, even though he uses this to fix the reference of his standard of length, a meter, he can still say, 'if heat had been applied to this stick $S$ at $t_0$, then at $t_0$ stick $S$ would not have been one meter long.'

Well, why can he do this? Part of the reason may lie in some people's minds in the philosophy of science, which I don't want to go into here. But a simple answer to the question is this: Even if this is the *only* standard of length that he uses,[20] there is an intuitive difference between the phrase 'one meter' and the phrase 'the length of $S$ at $t_0$'. The first phrase is meant to designate rigidly a certain length in all possible worlds, which in the actual world happens to be the length of the stick $S$ at $t_0$. On the other hand 'the length of $S$ at $t_0$' does not designate anything rigidly. In some counterfactual situations the stick might have been longer and in some shorter, if various stresses and strains had been applied to it. So we can say of this stick, the same way as we would of any other of the same substance and length, that if heat of a given quantity had been applied to it, it would have expanded to such and such a length. Such a

[20] Philosophers of science may see the key to the problem in a view that 'one meter' is a 'cluster concept'. I am asking the reader hypothetically to suppose that the 'definition' given is the *only* standard used to determine the metric system. I think the problem would still arise.

counterfactual statement, being true of other sticks with identical physical properties, will also be true of this stick. There is no conflict between that counterfactual statement and the definition of 'one meter' as 'the length of $S$ at $t_0$', because the 'definition', properly interpreted, does *not* say that the phrase 'one meter' is to be *synonymous* (even when talking about counterfactual situations) with the phrase 'the length of $S$ at $t_0$', but rather that we have *determined the reference* of the phrase 'one meter' by stipulating that 'one meter' is to be a *rigid* designator of the length which is in fact the length of $S$ at $t_0$. So this does *not* make it a necessary truth that $S$ is one meter long at $t_0$. In fact, under certain circumstances, $S$ would not have been one meter long. The reason is that one designator ('one meter') is rigid and the other designator ('the length of $S$ at $t_0$') is not.

What then, is the *epistemological* status of the statement 'Stick $S$ is one meter long at $t_0$', for someone who has fixed the metric system by reference to stick $S$? It would seem that he knows it *a priori*. For if he used stick $S$ to fix the reference of the term 'one meter', then as a result of this kind of 'definition' (which is not an abbreviative or synonymous definition), he knows automatically, without further investigation, that $S$ is one meter long.[21] On the other hand, even if $S$ is used as the standard of a meter, the *metaphysical* status of '$S$ is one meter long' will be that of a contingent statement, provided that 'one meter' is regarded as a rigid designator: under appropriate stresses and strains, heatings or coolings, $S$ would have had a length other than one meter even at $t_0$. (Such statements as 'Water boils at 100°C at sea level' can have a similar status.) So in this sense, there are contingent *a priori* truths. More important for present purposes, though, than accepting this

[21] Since the truth he knows is contingent, I choose *not* to call it 'analytic', stipulatively requiring analytic truths to be both necessary and *a priori*. See footnote 63.

example as an instance of the contingent *a priori*, is its illustration of the distinction between 'definitions' which fix a reference and those which give a synonym.

In the case of names one might make this distinction too. Suppose the reference of a name is given by a description or a cluster of descriptions. If the name *means the same* as that description or cluster of descriptions, it will not be a rigid designator. It will not necessarily designate the same object in all possible worlds, since other objects might have had the given properties in other possible worlds, unless (of course) we happened to use essential properties in our description. So suppose we say, 'Aristotle is the greatest man who studied with Plato'. If we used that as a *definition*, the name 'Aristotle' is to mean 'the greatest man who studied with Plato'. Then of course in some other possible world that man might not have studied with Plato and some other man would have been Aristotle. If, on the other hand, we merely use the description to *fix the referent* then that man will be the referent of 'Aristotle' in all possible worlds. The only use of the description will have been to pick out to which man we mean to refer. But then, when we say counterfactually 'suppose Aristotle had never gone into philosophy at all', we need not mean 'suppose a man who studied with Plato, and taught Alexander the Great, and wrote this and that, and so on, had never gone into philosophy at all', which might seem like a contradiction. We need only mean, 'suppose that *that man* had never gone into philosophy at all'.

It seems plausible to suppose that, in some cases, the reference of a name is indeed fixed *via* a description in the same way that the metric system was fixed. When the mythical agent first saw Hesperus, he may well have fixed his reference by saying, 'I shall use "Hesperus" as a name of the heavenly body appearing in yonder position in the sky.' He then fixed the reference of 'Hesperus' by its apparent celestial position. Does it follow that it is part of the *meaning* of the name that Hesperus has such and such position at the time in question? Surely not: if Hesperus had been hit earlier by a comet, it might have been visible at a different position at that time. In such a counterfactual situation we would say that Hesperus would not have occupied that position, but not that Hesperus would not have been Hesperus. The reason is that 'Hesperus' rigidly designates a certain heavenly body and 'the body in yonder position' does not—a different body, or no body might have been in that position, but no other body might have been Hesperus (though another body, not Hesperus, might have been *called* 'Hesperus'). Indeed, as I have said, I will hold that names are always rigid designators.

Frege and Russell certainly seem to have the full blown theory according to which a proper name is not a rigid designator and is synonymous with the description which replaced it. But another theory might be that this description is used to determine a rigid reference. These two alternatives will have different consequences for the questions I was asking before. If 'Moses' *means* 'the man who did such and such', then, if no one did such and such, Moses didn't exist; and maybe 'no one did such and such' is even an *analysis* of 'Moses didn't exist'. But if the description is used to fix a reference rigidly, then it's clear that that is *not* what is meant by 'Moses didn't exist', because we can ask, if we speak of a counterfactual case where no one did indeed do such and such, say, lead the Israelites out of Egypt, does it follow that, in such a situation, Moses wouldn't have existed? It would seem not. For surely Moses might have just decided to spend his days more pleasantly in the Egyptian courts. He might never have gone into either politics or religion at all; and in that case maybe no one would have done any of the things that the Bible relates of Moses. That doesn't in itself mean that in such a possible world Moses wouldn't have existed. If so, then

'Moses exists' means something different from 'the existence and uniqueness conditions for a certain description are fulfilled'; and therefore this does not give an analysis of the singular existential statement after all. If you give up the idea that this is a theory of meaning and make it into a theory of reference in the way that I have described, you give up some of the advantages of the theory. Singular existential statements and identity statements between names need some other analysis.

Frege should be criticized for using the term 'sense' in two senses. For he takes the sense of a designator to be its meaning; and he also takes it to be the way its reference is determined. Identifying the two, he supposes that both are given by definite descriptions. Ultimately, I will reject this second supposition too; but even were it right, I reject the first. A description may be used as synonymous with a designator, or it may be used to fix its reference. The two Fregean senses of 'sense' correspond to two senses of 'definition' in ordinary parlance. They should carefully be distinguished.[22]

[22] Usually the Fregean sense is now interpreted as the meaning, which must be carefully distinguished from a 'reference fixer'. We shall see below that for most speakers, unless they are the ones who initially give an object its name, the referent of the name is determined by a 'causal' chain of communication rather than a description.

In the formal semantics of modal logic, the 'sense' of a term $t$ is usually taken to be the (possibly partial) function which assigns to each possible world $H$ the referent of $t$ in $H$. For a rigid designator, such a function is constant. This notion of 'sense' relates to that of 'giving a meaning', not that of fixing a reference. In this use of 'sense', 'one meter' has a constant function as its sense, though its reference is fixed by 'the length of $S$', which does not have a constant function as its sense.

Some philosophers have thought that descriptions, in English, are ambiguous, that sometimes they non-rigidly designate, in each world, the object (if any) satisfying the description, while sometimes they *rigidly* designate the object actually satisfying the description. (Others, inspired by Donnellan, say the description sometimes rigidly designates the object thought or presupposed to satisfy the description.) I find any such alleged ambiguities dubious. I know

I hope the idea of fixing the reference as opposed to actually defining one term as meaning the other is somewhat clear. There is really not enough time to go into everything in great detail. I think, even in cases where the notion of rigidity versus accidentality of designation cannot be used to make out the difference in question, some things called definitions really intend to fix a reference rather than to give the meaning of a phrase, to give a synonym. Let me give an example. $\pi$ is supposed to be the ratio of the circumference of a circle to its diameter. Now, it's something that I have nothing but a vague intuitive feeling to argue for: It seems to me that here this Greek letter is not being used as *short for* the phrase 'the ratio of the circumference of a circle to its diameter' nor is it even used as short for a cluster of alternative definitions of $\pi$, whatever that might mean. It is used as a *name* for a real number, which in this case is necessarily the ratio of the circumference of a circle to its diameter. Note that here both '$\pi$' and 'the ratio of the circumference of a circle to its diameter' are rigid designators, so the arguments given in the metric case are inapplicable. (Well, if someone doesn't see this, or thinks it's wrong, it doesn't matter.)

Let me return to the question about names which I raised. As I said, there is a popular modern substitute for the theory of Frege and Russell; it is adopted even by such a strong critic of many views of Frege and Russell, especially the latter, as

---

of no clear evidence for them which cannot be handled either by Russell's notion of scope or by the considerations alluded to in footnote 3, p. 25.

If the ambiguity does exist, then in the supposed *rigid* sense of 'the length of *S*', 'one meter' and 'the length of *S*' designate the same thing in all possible worlds and have the same (functional) 'sense'.

In the formal semantics of intensional logic, suppose we take a definite description to designate, in each world, the object satisfying the description. It is indeed useful to have an operator which transforms each description into a term which rigidly designates the object *actually* satisfying the description. David Kaplan has proposed such an operator and calls it 'Dthat'.

Strawson.[23] The substitute is that, although a name is not a disguised description it either abbreviates, or anyway its reference is determined by, some cluster of descriptions. The question is whether this is true. As I also said, there are stronger and weaker versions of this. The stronger version would say that the name is simply *defined*, synonymously, as the cluster of descriptions. It will then be necessary, not that Moses had any particular property in this cluster, but that he had the disjunction of them. There couldn't be any counterfactual situation in which he didn't do any of those things. I think it's clear that this is very implausible. People *have* said it—or maybe they haven't been intending to say that, but were using 'necessary' in some other sense. At any rate, for example, in Searle's article on proper names:

> To put the same point differently, suppose we ask, 'why do we have proper names at all?' Obviously to refer to individuals. 'Yes but descriptions could do that for us'. But only at the cost of specifying identity conditions every time reference is made: Suppose we agree to drop 'Aristotle' and use, say, 'the teacher of Alexander', then it is a necessary truth that the man referred to is Alexander's teacher—but it is a contingent fact that Aristotle ever went into pedagogy (though I am suggesting that it is a necessary fact that Aristotle has the logical sum, inclusive disjunction, of properties commonly attributed to him).[24]

Such a suggestion, if 'necessary' is used in the way I have been using it in this lecture, must clearly be false. (Unless he's got some very interesting essential property commonly attributed to Aristotle.) Most of the things commonly attributed to Aristotle are things that Aristotle might not have done at all. In a situation in which he didn't do them, we would describe that as a situation in which *Aristotle* didn't do them. This is not a distinction of scope, as happens sometimes in the case of

[23] P. F. Strawson, *Individuals*, Methuen, London, 1959, Ch. 6.

[24] Searle, op. cit. in Caton, *Philosophy and Ordinary Language*, p. 160.

descriptions, where someone might say that the man who taught Alexander might not have taught Alexander; though it could not have been true that: the man who taught Alexander didn't teach Alexander. This is Russell's distinction of scope. (I won't go into it.) It seems to me clear that this is not the case here. Not only is it true *of* the man Aristotle that he might not have gone into pedagogy; it is also true that we use the term 'Aristotle' in such a way that, in thinking of a counterfactual situation in which Aristotle didn't go into any of the fields and do any of the achievements we commonly attribute to him, still we would say that was a situation in which *Aristotle* did not do these things.[25] Well there are some things like the date, the period he lived in, that might be more imagined as necessary. Maybe those are things we commonly attribute to him. There are exceptions. Maybe it's hard to imagine how he could have lived 500 years later than he in fact did. That certainly raises at least a problem. But take a man who doesn't have any idea of the date. Many people just have some vague cluster of his most famous achievements. Not only each of these singly, but the possession of the entire disjunction of these properties, is just a contingent fact about Aristotle; and the statement

[25] The facts that 'the teacher of Alexander' is capable of scope distinctions in modal contexts and that it is not a rigid designator are both illustrated when one observes that the teacher of Alexander might not have taught Alexander (and, in such circumstances, would not have been the teacher of Alexander). On the other hand, it is not true that Aristotle might not have been Aristotle, although Aristotle might not have been *called* 'Aristotle', just as 2 × 2 might not have been *called* 'four'. (Sloppy, colloquial speech, which often confuses use and mention, may, of course, express the fact that someone might have been called, or not have been called, 'Aristotle' by saying that he might have been, or not have been, Aristotle. Occasionally, I have heard such loose usages adduced as counterexamples to the applicability of the present theory to ordinary language. Colloquialisms like these seem to me to create as little problem for my theses as the success of the 'Impossible Missions Force' creates for the modal law that the impossible does not happen.) Further, although under certain circumstances Aristotle would not have taught Alexander, these are not circumstances under which he would not have been Aristotle.

that Aristotle had this disjunction of properties is a contingent truth.

A man might know it *a priori* in some sense, if he in fact fixes the reference of 'Aristotle' as the man who did one of these things. Still it won't be a necessary truth for him. So this sort of example would be an example where a prioricity would not necessarily imply necessity, if the cluster theory of names were right. The case of fixing the reference of 'one meter' is a very clear example in which someone, just because he fixed the reference in this way, can in some sense know *a priori* that the length of this stick is a meter without regarding it as a necessary truth. Maybe the thesis about a prioricity implying necessity can be modified. It does appear to state some insight which might be important, and true, about epistemology. In a way an example like this may seem like a trivial counterexample which is not really the point of what some people think when they think that only necessary truths can be known *a priori*. Well, if the thesis that all *a priori* truth is necessary is to be immune from this sort of counterexample, it needs to be modified in some way. Unmodified it leads to confusion about the nature of reference. And I myself have no idea how it should be modified or restated, or if such a modification or restatement is possible.[26]

[26] If someone fixes a meter as 'the length of stick $S$ at $t_0$', then in some sense he knows *a priori* that the length of stick $S$ at $t_0$ is one meter, even though he uses this statement to express a contingent truth. But, merely by fixing a system of measurement, has he thereby *learned* some (contingent) *information* about the world, some new *fact* that he did not know before? It seems plausible that in some sense he did not, even though it is undeniably a contingent fact that $S$ is one meter long. So there may be a case for reformulating the thesis that everything *a priori* is necessary so as to save it from this type of counterexample. As I said, I don't know how such a reformulation would go; the reformulation should not be such as to make the thesis trivial (e.g., by defining *a priori* as known to be *necessary* (instead of true) independently of experience); and the converse thesis would still be false.

Since I will not attempt such a reformulation, I shall consistently use the

Let me state then what the cluster concept theory of names is. (It really is a nice theory. The only defect I think it has is probably common to all philosophical theories. It's wrong. You may suspect me of proposing another theory in its place; but I hope not, because I'm sure it's wrong too if it is a theory.) The theory in question can be broken down into a number of theses, with some subsidiary theses if you want to see how it handles the problem of existence statements, identity statements, and so on. There are more theses if you take it in the stronger version as a theory of meaning. The speaker is *A*.

(1) To every name or designating expression '*X*', there corresponds a cluster of properties, namely the family of properties $\varphi$ such that *A* believes '$\varphi X$'.

This thesis is true, because it can just be a definition. Now, of course, some people might think that not everything the speaker believes about *X* has anything to do with determining the reference of '*X*'. They might only be interested in a subset. But we can handle this later on by modifying some of the other theses. So this thesis is correct, by definition. The theses that follow, however, are all, I think, false.

(2) One of the properties, or some conjointly, are believed by *A* to pick out some individual uniquely.

This doesn't say that they do pick out something uniquely, just that *A* believes that they do. Another thesis is that he is correct.

(3) If most, or a weighted most, of the $\varphi$'s are satisfied by one unique object *y*, then *y* is the referent of '*X*'.

Well, the theory says that the referent of '*X*' is supposed to be the thing satisfying, if not all the properties, 'enough' of them.

term '*a priori*' in the text so as to make statements whose truth follows from a reference-fixing 'definition' *a priori*.

Obviously *A* could be wrong about some things about *X*. You take some sort of a vote. Now the question is whether this vote should be democratic or have some inequalities among the properties. It seems more plausible that there should be some weighting, that some properties are more important than others. A theory really has to specify how this weighting goes. I believe that Strawson, to my surprise, explicitly states that democracy should rule here, so the most trivial properties are of equal weight with the most crucial.[27] Surely it is more plausible to suppose that there is some weighting. Let's say democracy doesn't necessarily rule. If there is any property that's completely irrelevant to the reference we can disenfranchise it altogether, by giving it weight 0. The properties can be regarded as members of a corporation. Some have more stock than others; some may even have only non-voting stock.

(4) If the vote yields no unique object, '*X*' does not refer.

(5) The statement, 'If *X* exists, then *X* has most of the φ's' is known *a priori* by the speaker.

(6) The statement, 'If *X* exists, then *X* has most of the φ's' expresses a necessary truth (in the idiolect of the speaker).

(6) need not be a thesis of the theory if someone doesn't think that the cluster is part of the meaning of the name. He could think that though he determines the reference of 'Aristotle' as the man who had most of the φ's, still there are certainly possible situations in which Aristotle wouldn't have had most of the φ's.

As I indicated, there are some subsidiary theses, though I won't go into them in detail. These would give the analyses of singular existential statements like, '"Moses exists" means

[27] Strawson, op. cit., pp. 191–92. Strawson actually considers the case of several speakers, pools their properties, and takes a democratic (equally weighted) vote. He requires only a sufficiently plurality, not a majority.

"enough of the properties φ are satisfied" '. Even the man who doesn't use the theory as a theory of meaning has some of these theses. For example, subsidiary to thesis 4, we should say that it is *a priori* true for the speaker that, if not enough of the φ's are satisfied, then *X* does not exist. Only if he holds the view as a theory of meaning, rather than of reference, would it also be *necessarily* true that, if not enough of the φ's are satisfied, *X* does not exist. In any case it will be something he knows *a priori*. (At least he will know it *a priori* provided he knows the proper theory of names.) Then there is also an analysis of identity statements along the same lines.

The question is, are any of these true? If true, they give a nice picture of what's going on. Preliminary to discussing these theses, let me mention that, often, when people specify which properties φ are relevant, they seem to specify them wrongly. That's just an incidental defect, though it is closely related to the arguments against the theory that I will give presently. Consider the example from Wittgenstein. What does he say the relevant properties are? 'When one says "Moses does not exist", this may mean various things. It may mean: the Israelites did not have a *single* leader when they withdrew from Egypt—or: their leader was not called Moses—or: there cannot have been anyone who accomplished all that the Bible relates of Moses. . . .' The gist of all this is that we know *a priori* that, if the Biblical story is substantially false, Moses did not exist. I have already argued that the Biblical story does not give *necessary* properties of Moses, that he might have lived without doing any of these things. Here I ask whether we know *a priori* that if Moses existed, he in fact did some or most of them. Is this really the cluster of properties that we should use here? Surely there is a distinction which is neglected in these kinds of remarks. The Biblical story might have been a complete legend, or it might have been a substantially false account of a real person. In the latter case, it seems to me that a scholar could say that he supposes that, though Moses did exist, the things said of him in the Bible are substantially false. Such things occur in this very field of scholarship. Suppose that someone says that no prophet ever was swallowed by a big fish or a whale. Does it follow, on that basis, that Jonah did not exist? There still seems to be the question whether the Biblical account is a legendary account of no person or a legendary account built on a real person. In the latter case, it's only natural to say that, though Jonah did exist, no one did the things commonly related to him. I choose this case because while Biblical scholars generally hold that Jonah did exist, the account not only of his being swallowed by a big fish but even going to Nineveh to preach or anything else that is said in the Biblical story is assumed to be substantially false. But nevertheless there are reasons for thinking this was about a real prophet. If I had a suitable book along with me I could start quoting out of it: 'Jonah, the son of Amittai, was a real prophet, however such and such and such'. There are independent reasons for thinking this was not a pure legend about an imaginary character but one about a real character.[28]

[28] See, for example, H. L. Ginsberg, *The Five Megilloth and Jonah*, The Jewish Publication Society of America, 1969, p. 114: 'The "hero" of this tale, the prophet Jonah the son of Amittai, is a historical personage . . . (but) this book is not history but fiction.' The scholarly consensus regards all details about Jonah in the book as legendary and not even based on a factual substratum, excepting the bare statement that he was a Hebrew prophet, which is hardly uniquely identifying. Nor need he have been *called* 'Jonah' by the Hebrews; the '*J*' sound does not exist in Hebrew, and Jonah's historical existence is independent of whether we know his original Hebrew name or not. The fact that *we* call him Jonah cannot be used to single him out without circularity. The evidence for the historicity of Jonah comes from an independent reference to him in *II Kings*; but such evidence could have been available in the absence of any such other references—e.g., evidence that all Hebrew legends were about actual personages. Further, the statement that Jonah is a legend about a real person might have been *true*, even if there were no evidence for it. One may say, 'The Jonah of the book never existed,' as one may say, 'The Hitler of Nazi propaganda never existed.' As the quotation above shows, this usage

These examples could be modified. Maybe all we believe is that *the Bible relates of him* that such and such. This gives us another problem, because how do we know whom the Bible is referring to? The question of our reference is thrown back to the question of reference in the Bible. This leads to a condition which we ought to put in explicitly.

(C) For any successful theory, the account must not be circular. The properties which are used in the vote must not themselves involve the notion of reference in a way that it is ultimately impossible to eliminate.

Let me give an example where the noncircularity condition is clearly violated. The following theory of proper names is due to William Kneale in an article called 'Modality, De Dicto and De Re'.[29] It contains, I think, a clear violation of noncircularity conditions.

Ordinary proper names of people are not, as John Stuart Mill supposed, signs without sense. While it may be informative to tell a man that the most famous Greek philosopher was called Socrates, it is obviously trifling to tell him that Socrates was called Socrates; and the reason is simply that he cannot understand your use of the word 'Socrates' at the beginning of your statement unless he already knows that 'Socrates' means 'The individual called "Socrates"'.[30]

Here we have a theory of the reference of proper names. 'Socrates' just means 'the man called "Socrates".' Actually, of course, maybe not just one man can be called 'Socrates', and

---

need not coincide with the historian's view of whether Jonah ever existed. Ginsberg is writing for the lay reader, who, he assumes, will find his statement intelligible.

[29] In Ernest Nagel, Patrick Suppes, and Alfred Tarski, *Logic, Methodology and the Philosophy of Science: Proceedings of the 1960 International Congress*, Stanford University Press, 1962, 622–33.

[30] *Loc. cit.*, pp. 629–30.

some may call him 'Socrates' while others may not. Certainly that is a condition which under some circumstances is uniquely satisfied. Maybe only one man was called 'Socrates' by me on a certain occasion.

Kneale says it's trifling to tell someone that Socrates *was* called 'Socrates'. That isn't trifling on any view. Maybe the Greeks didn't call him 'Socrates'. Let's say that Socrates is called 'Socrates' by us—by *me* anyway. Suppose that's trifling. (I find it surprising that Kneale uses the past tense here; it is dubious that the Greeks *did* call him 'Socrates'—at least, the Greek name is pronounced differently. I will check the accuracy of the quotation for the next lecture.)

Kneale gives an argument for this theory. 'Socrates' must be analyzed as 'the individual called "Socrates" ', because how else can we explain the fact that it is trifling to be told that Socrates is called 'Socrates'? In some cases that's rather trifling. In the same sense, I suppose, you could get a good theory of the meaning of any expression in English and construct a dictionary. For example, though it may be informative to tell someone that horses are used in races, it is trifling to tell him that horses are called 'horses'. Therefore this could only be the case because the term 'horse', means in English 'the things called "horses" '. Similarly with any other expression which might be used in English. Since it's trifling to be told that sages are called 'sages', 'sages' just means 'the people called "sages" '. Now plainly this isn't really a very good argument, nor can it therefore be the only explanation of why it's trifling to be told that Socrates is called 'Socrates'. Let's not go into exactly why it's trifling. Of course, anyone who knows the use of 'is called' in English, even without knowing what the statement means, knows that if 'quarks' means something then 'quarks are called "quarks" ' will express a truth. He may not know what truth it expresses, because he doesn't know what a quark is. But his knowledge that it expresses a truth does not have much to do with the meaning of the term 'quarks'.

We could go into this actually at great length. There are interesting problems coming out of this sort of passage. But the main reason I wanted to introduce it here is that as a theory of reference it would give a clear violation of the noncircularity condition. Someone uses the name 'Socrates'. How are we supposed to know to whom he refers? By using the description which gives the sense of it. According to Kneale, the description is 'the man called "Socrates"'. And here, (presumably, since this is supposed to be so trifling!) it tells us nothing at all. Taking it in this way it seems to be no theory of reference at all. We ask, 'To whom does he refer by "Socrates"?' And then the answer is given, 'Well, he refers to the man to whom he refers.' If this were all there was to the meaning of a proper name, then no reference would get off the ground at all.

So there's a condition to be satisfied; in the case of this particular theory it's obviously unsatisfied. The paradigm, amazingly enough, is even sometimes used by Russell as the descriptive sense, namely: 'the man called "Walter Scott"'. Obviously if the only descriptive senses of names we can think of are of the form 'the man called such and such', 'the man called "Walter Scott"', 'the man called "Socrates"', then whatever this relation of *calling* is is really what determines the reference and not any description like 'the man called "Socrates"'.

# LECTURE II: JANUARY 22, 1970

Last time we ended up talking about a theory of naming which is given by a number of theses here on the board.

(1) To every name or designating expression '$X$', there corresponds a cluster of properties, namely the family of those properties $\varphi$ such that $A$ believes '$\varphi X$'.

(2) One of the properties, or some conjointly, are believed by $A$ to pick out some individual uniquely.

(3) If most, or a weighted most, of the $\varphi$'s are satisfied by one unique object $y$, then $y$ is the referent of '$X$'.

(4) If the vote yields no unique object, '$X$' does not refer.

(5) The statement, 'If $X$ exists, then $X$ has most of the $\varphi$'s' is known *a priori* by the speaker.

(6) The statement, 'If $X$ exists, then $X$ has most of the $\varphi$'s' expresses a necessary truth (in the idiolect of the speaker).

(C) For any successful theory, the account must not be circular. The properties which are used in the vote must not themselves involve the notion of reference in such a way that it is ultimately impossible to eliminate.

(C) is not a thesis but a condition on the satisfaction of the other theses. In other words, Theses (1)–(6) cannot be satisfied in a way which leads to a circle, in a way which does not lead to any independent determination of reference. The example I gave last time of a blatantly circular attempt to satisfy these conditions was a theory of names mentioned by William Kneale. I was a little surprised at the statement of the theory when I was reading what I had copied down, so I looked it up again. I looked it up in the book to see if I'd copied it down accurately. Kneale *did* use the past tense. He said that though it is not trifling to be told that Socrates was the greatest philosopher of ancient Greece, it is trifling to be told that Socrates was called 'Socrates'. Therefore, he concludes, the name 'Socrates' must simply mean 'the individual called "Socrates" '. Russell, as I've said, in some places gives a similar analysis. Anyway, as stated using the past tense, the condition wouldn't be circular, because one certainly could decide to use the term 'Socrates' to refer to whoever was called 'Socrates' by the Greeks. But, of course, in that sense it's not at all trifling to be told that Socrates was called 'Socrates'. If this is any kind of fact, it might be false. Perhaps we know that *we* call him 'Socrates'; that hardly shows that the Greeks did so. In fact, of course, they may have pronounced the name differently. It may be, in the case of this particular name, that transliteration from the Greek is so good that the English version is not pronounced *very* differently from the Greek. But that won't be so in the general case. Certainly it is not trifling to be told that Isaiah was called 'Isaiah'. In fact, it is false to be told that Isaiah was called 'Isaiah'; the prophet wouldn't have recognized this name at all. And of course the Greeks didn't call their country anything like 'Greece'. Suppose we amend the thesis so that it reads: it's trifling to be told that Socrates is called 'Socrates' by us, or at least, by me, the speaker. Then in some sense this is fairly trifling. I don't think it is necessary or analytic. In the same way, it is trifling to be told that horses are called 'horses', without this leading to the conclusion that the word 'horse' simply *means* 'the animal called a "horse" '. As a theory of the reference of the name 'Socrates' it will lead immediately to a vicious circle. If one was determining the referent of a name like 'Glunk' to himself and made the following decision, 'I shall use the term "Glunk" to refer to the man that I call "Glunk" ', this would get one nowhere. One had better have some independent determination of the referent of 'Glunk'. This is a good example of a blatantly circular determination. Actually sentences like 'Socrates is called "Socrates" ' are very interesting and one can spend, strange as it may seem, hours talking about their analysis. I actually did, once, do that. I won't do that, however, on this occasion. (See how high the seas of language can rise. And at the lowest points too.) Anyway this is a useful example of a violation of the noncircularity condition. The theory will satisfy all of these statements, perhaps, but it satisfies them only because there is some independent way of determining the reference independently of the particular condition: being the man called 'Socrates'.

I have already talked about, in the last lecture, Thesis (6). Theses (5) and (6), by the way, have converses. What I said for Thesis (5) is that the statement that if $X$ exists, $X$ has most of the $\varphi$'s, is *a priori* true for the speaker. It will also be true under the given theory that certain converses of this statement hold true also *a priori* for the speaker, namely: if any unique thing has most of the properties $\varphi$ in the properly weighted sense, it is $X$. Similarly a certain converse to this will be *necessarily* true, namely: if anything has most of the properties $\varphi$ in the properly weighted sense, it is $X$. So really one can say that it is both *a priori* and necessary that something is $X$ if and only if it uniquely has most of the properties $\varphi$. This really comes from the previous Theses (1)–(4), I suppose. And (5) and (6) really just say that a sufficiently reflective speaker grasps this theory of proper names. Knowing this, he therefore sees that (5) and (6) are true. The objections to Theses (5) and (6) will *not* be that some speakers are unaware of this theory and therefore don't know these things.

What I talked about in the last lecture is Thesis (6). It's been observed by many philosophers that, if the cluster of properties associated with a proper name is taken in a very narrow sense, so that only one property is given any weight at all, let's say one definite description to pick out the referent—for example, Aristotle was the philosopher who taught Alexander the Great—then certain things will seem to turn out to be necessary truths which are not necessary truths—in this case, for example, that Aristotle taught Alexander the Great. But as Searle said, it is not a necessary truth but a contingent one that Aristotle ever went into pedagogy. Therefore, he concludes that one must drop the original paradigm of a single description and turn to that of a cluster of descriptions.

To summarize some things that I argued last time, this is not the correct answer (whatever it may be) to this problem about necessity. For Searle goes on to say,

> Suppose we agree to drop 'Aristotle' and use, say, 'the teacher of Alexander', then it is a necessary truth that the man referred to is Alexander's teacher—but it is a contingent fact that Aristotle ever went into pedagogy, though I am suggesting that it is a necessary fact that Aristotle has the logical sum, inclusive disjunction, of properties commonly attributed to him. . . .[31]

This is what is not so. It just is not, in any intuitive sense of necessity, a necessary truth that Aristotle had the properties commonly attributed to him. There is a certain theory, perhaps popular in some views of the philosophy of history, which might both be deterministic and yet at the same time assign a great role to the individual in history. Perhaps Carlyle would associate with the meaning of the name of a great man his achievements. According to such a view it will be necessary, once a certain individual is born, that he is destined to perform

[31] Searle, 'Proper Names', in Caton, op. cit., p. 160.

various great tasks and so it will be part of the very nature of Aristotle that he should have produced ideas which had a great influence on the western world. Whatever the merits of such a view may be as a view of history or the nature of great men, it does not seem that it should be trivially true on the basis of a theory of proper names. It would seem that it's a contingent fact that Aristotle ever did *any* of the things commonly attributed to him today, *any* of these great achievements that we so much admire. I must say that there is *something* to this feeling of Searle's. When I hear the name 'Hitler', I do get an illusory 'gut feeling' that it's sort of analytic that that man was evil. But really, probably not. Hitler might have spent all his days in quiet in Linz. In that case we would not say that then this man would not have been Hitler, for we use the name 'Hitler' just as the name of that man, even in describing other possible worlds. (This is the notion which I called a *rigid designator* in the previous talk.) Suppose we do decide to pick out the reference of 'Hitler', as the man who succeeded in having more Jews killed than anyone else managed to do in history. That is the way we pick out the reference of the name; but in another counterfactual situation where some one else would have gained this discredit, we wouldn't say that in that case that other man would have been Hitler. If Hitler had never come to power, Hitler would not have had the property which I am supposing we use to fix the reference of his name. Similarly, even if we define what a meter is by reference to the standard meter stick, it will be a contingent truth and not a necessary one that that particular stick is one meter long. If it had been stretched, it would have been longer than one meter. And that is because we use the term 'one meter' rigidly to designate a certain length. Even though we fix what length we are designating by an accidental property of that length, just as in the case of the name of the man we may pick the man out by an accidental property of the man, still we use the name to designate that man or that length in all possible worlds. The property we use need not be one which is regarded in any way as necessary or essential. In the case of a yard, the original way this length was picked out was, I think, the distance when the arm of King Henry I of England was outstretched from the tip of his finger to his nose. If this was the length of a yard, it nevertheless will not be a necessary truth that the distance between the tip of his finger and his nose should be a yard. Maybe an accident might have happened to foreshorten his arm; that would be possible. And the reason that it's not a necessary truth is not that there might be other criteria in a 'cluster concept' of yardhood. Even a man who strictly uses King Henry's arm as his one standard of length can say, counterfactually, that if certain things had happened to the King, the exact distance between the end of one of his fingers and his nose would not have been exactly a yard. He need not be using a cluster as long as he uses the term 'yard' to pick out a certain fixed reference to be that length in all possible worlds.

These remarks show, I think, the intuitive bizarreness of a good deal of the literature on 'transworld identification' and 'counterpart theory'. For many theorists of these sorts, believing, as they do, that a 'possible world' is given to us only qualitatively, argue that Aristotle is to be 'identified in other possible worlds', or alternatively that his counterparts are to be identified, with those things in other possible worlds who most closely resemble Aristotle in his most important properties. (Lewis, for example, says: 'Your counterparts . . . resemble you . . . in important respects . . . more closely than do the other things in their worlds . . . weighted by the importance of the various respects and by the degrees of the similarities.'[32]) Some may equate the important properties with those

[32] D. Lewis, op. cit., pp. 114–15.

properties used to identify the object in the actual world.

Surely these notions are incorrect. To me Aristotle's most important properties consist in his philosophical work, and Hitler's in his murderous political role; both, as I have said, might have lacked these properties altogether. Surely there was no logical fate hanging over either Aristotle or Hitler which made it in any sense inevitable that they should have possessed the properties we regard as important to them; they could have had careers completely different from their actual ones. *Important* properties of an object need not be essential, unless 'importance' is used as a synonym for essence; and an object could have had properties very different from its most striking actual properties, or from the properties we use to identify it.

To clear up one thing which some people have asked me: When I say that a designator is rigid, and designates the same thing in all possible worlds, I mean that, as used in *our* language, it stands for that thing, when *we* talk about counterfactual situations. I don't mean, of course, that there mightn't be counterfactual situations in which in the other possible worlds people actually spoke a different language. One doesn't say that 'two plus two equals four' is contingent because people might have spoken a language in which 'two plus two equals four' meant that seven is even. Similarly, when we speak of a counterfactual situation, we speak of it in English, even if it is part of the description of that counterfactual situation that we were all speaking German in that counterfactual situation. We say, 'suppose we had all been speaking German' or 'suppose we had been using English in a nonstandard way'. Then we are describing a possible world or counterfactual situation in which people, including ourselves, did speak in a certain way different from the way we speak. But still, in describing that world, we use *English* with *our* meanings and *our* references. It is in this sense that I speak of a rigid designator as having the same reference in all possible worlds. I also don't mean to imply that the thing designated exists in all possible worlds, just that the name refers rigidly to that thing. If you say 'suppose Hitler had never been born' then 'Hitler' refers here, still rigidly, to something that would not exist in the counterfactual situation described.

Given these remarks, this means we must cross off Thesis (6) as incorrect. The other theses have nothing to do with necessity and can survive. In particular Thesis (5) has nothing to do with necessity and it can survive. If I use the name 'Hesperus' to refer to a certain planetary body when seen in a certain celestial position in the evening, it will not therefore be a necessary truth that Hesperus is ever seen in the evening. That depends on various contingent facts about people being there to see and things like that. So even if I should say to myself that I will use 'Hesperus' to name the heavenly body I see in the evening in yonder position of the sky, it will not be necessary that Hesperus was ever seen in the evening. But it may be *a priori* in that this is how I have determined the referent. If I have determined that Hesperus is the thing that I saw in the evening over there, then I will know, just from making that determination of the referent, that if there is any Hesperus at all it's the thing I saw in the evening. This at least survives as far as the arguments we have given up to now go.

How about a theory where Thesis (6) is eliminated? Theses (2), (3), and (4) turn out to have a large class of counterinstances. Even when Theses (2)–(4) are true, Thesis (5) is usually false; the truth of Theses (3) and (4) is an empirical 'accident', which the speaker hardly knows *a priori*. That is to say, other principles really determine the speaker's reference, and the fact that the referent coincides with that determined by (2)–(4) is an 'accident', which we were in no position to know *a priori*. Only in a rare class of cases, usually initial baptisms, are all of (2)–(5) true.

What picture of naming do these Theses ((1)–(5)) give you? The picture is this. I want to name an object. I think of some way of describing it uniquely and then I go through, so to speak, a sort of mental ceremony: By 'Cicero' I shall mean the man who denounced Catiline; and that's what the reference of 'Cicero' will be. I will use 'Cicero' to designate rigidly the man who (in fact) denounced Catiline, so I can speak of possible worlds in which he did not. But still my intentions are given by first, giving some condition which uniquely determines an object, then using a certain word as a name for the object determined by this condition. Now there may be some cases in which we actually do this. Maybe, if you want to stretch and call it description, when you say: I shall call that heavenly body over there 'Hesperus'.[33] That is really a case where the theses not only are true but really even give a correct picture of how the reference is determined. Another case, if you want to call this a name, might be when the police in London use the name 'Jack' or 'Jack the Ripper' to refer to the man, whoever he is, who committed all these murders, or most of them. Then they are giving the reference of the name

[33] An even better case of determining the reference of a name by description, as opposed to ostension, is the discovery of the planet Neptune. Neptune was hypothesized as the planet which caused such and such discrepancies in the orbits of certain other planets. If Leverrier indeed gave the name 'Neptune' to the planet before it was ever seen, then he fixed the reference of 'Neptune' by means of the description just mentioned. At that time he was unable to see the planet even through a telescope. At this stage, an *a priori* material equivalence held between the statements 'Neptune exists' and 'some one planet perturbing the orbit of such and such other planets exists in such and such a position', and also such statements as 'if such and such perturbations are caused by a planet, they are caused by Neptune' had the status of *a priori* truths. Nevertheless, they were not *necessary* truths, since 'Neptune' was introduced as a name rigidly designating a certain planet. Leverrier could well have believed that if Neptune had been knocked off its course one million years earlier, it would have caused no such perturbations and even that some other object might have caused the perturbations in its place.

by a description.[34] But in many or most cases, I think the theses are false. So let's look at them.[35]

Thesis (1), as I say, is a definition. Thesis (2) says that one of the properties believed by *A* of the object, or some conjointly, are believed to pick out some individual uniquely. A sort of example people have in mind is just what I said: I shall use the term 'Cicero' to denote the man who denounced Catiline (or first denounced him in public, to make it unique). This picks out an object uniquely in this particular reference. Even some writers such as Ziff in *Semantic Analysis*, who don't believe that names have meaning in any sense, think that this is a good picture of the way reference can be determined.

Let's see if Thesis (2) is true. It seems, in some *a priori* way, that it's got to be true, because if you don't think that the properties you have in mind pick out anyone uniquely—let's say they're all satisfied by two people—then how can you say which one of them you're talking about? There seem to be no grounds for saying you're talking about the one rather than about the other. Usually the properties in question are supposed to be some famous deeds of the person in question. For example, Cicero was the man who denounced Catiline. The average person, according to this, when he refers to Cicero, is

[34] Following Donnellan's remarks on definite descriptions, we should add that in some cases, an object may be identified, and the reference of a name fixed, using a description which may turn out to be false of its object. The case where the reference of 'Phosphorus' is determined as the 'morning star', which later turns out not to be a star, is an obvious example. In such cases, the description which fixes the reference clearly is in no sense known *a priori* to hold of the object, though a more cautious substitute may be. If such a more cautious substitute is available, it is really the substitute which fixes the reference in the sense intended in the text.

[35] Some of the theses are sloppily stated in respect of fussy matters like use of quotation marks and related details. (For example, Theses (5) and (6), as stated, presuppose that the speaker's language is English.) Since the purport of the theses is clear, and they are false anyway, I have not bothered to set these things straight.

saying something like 'the man who denounced Catiline' and thus has picked out a certain man uniquely. It is a tribute to the education of philosophers that they have held this thesis for such a long time. In fact, most people, when they think of Cicero, just think of *a famous Roman orator*, without any pretension to think either that there was only one famous Roman orator or that one must know something else about Cicero to have a referent for the name. Consider Richard Feynman, to whom many of us are able to refer. He is a leading contemporary theoretical physicist. Everyone *here* (I'm sure!) can state the contents of one of Feynman's theories so as to differentiate him from Gell-Mann. However, the man in the street, not possessing these abilities, may still use the name 'Feynman'. When asked he will say: well he's a physicist or something. He may not think that this picks out anyone uniquely. I still think he uses the name 'Feynman' as a name for Feynman.

But let's look at some of the cases where we do have a description to pick out someone uniquely. Let's say, for example, that we know that Cicero was the man who first denounced Catiline. Well, that's good. That really picks someone out uniquely. However, there is a problem, because this description contains another name, namely 'Catiline'. We must be sure that we satisfy the conditions in such a way as to avoid violating the noncircularity condition here. In particular, we must not say that Catiline was the man denounced by Cicero. If we do this, we will really not be picking out anything uniquely, we will simply be picking out a pair of objects *A* and *B*, such that *A* denounced *B*. We do not think that this was the only pair where such denunciations ever occurred; so we had better add some other conditions in order to satisfy the uniqueness condition.

If we say Einstein was the man who discovered the theory of relativity, that certainly picks out someone uniquely. One can be sure, as I said, that everyone *here* can make a compact and independent statement of this theory and so pick out Einstein uniquely; but many people actually don't know enough about this stuff, so when asked what the theory of relativity is, they will say: 'Einstein's theory', and thus be led into the most straightforward sort of vicious circle.

So Thesis (2), in a straightforward way, fails to be satisfied when we say Feynman is a famous physicist without attributing anything else to Feynman. In another way it may not be satisfied in the proper way even when it is satisfied: If we say Einstein was 'the man who discovered relativity theory', that does pick someone out uniquely; but it may not pick him out in such a way as to satisfy the noncircularity condition, because the theory of relativity may in turn be picked out as 'Einstein's theory'. So Thesis (2) seems to be false.

By changing the conditions φ from those usually associated with names by philosophers, one could try to improve the theory. There have been various ways I've heard; maybe I'll discuss these later on. Usually they think of famous achievements of the man named. Certainly in the case of famous achievements, the theory doesn't work. Some student of mine once said, 'Well, Einstein discovered the theory of relativity'; and he determined the reference of 'the theory of relativity' independently by referring to an encyclopedia which would give the details of the theory. (This is what is called a transcendental deduction of the existence of encyclopedias.) But it seems to me that, even if someone has heard of encyclopedias, it really is not essential for his reference that he should know whether this theory is given in detail in any encyclopedia. The reference might work even if there had been no encyclopedias at all.

Let's go on to Thesis (3): If most of the φ's, suitably weighted, are satisfied by a unique object *y*, then *y* is the referent of the name for the speaker. Now, since we have already established that Thesis (2) is wrong, why should any of the rest work? The whole theory depended on always being able to specify unique conditions which are satisfied. But still we can look at the other theses. The picture associated with the theory is that only by giving some unique properties can you know who someone is and thus know what the reference of your name is. Well, I won't go into the question of knowing who someone is. It's really very puzzling. I think you *do* know who Cicero is if you just can answer that he's a famous Roman orator. Strangely enough, if you know that Einstein discovered the theory of relativity and nothing about that theory, you can both know who Einstein is, namely the discoverer of the theory of relativity, and who discovered the theory of relativity, namely Einstein, on the basis of this knowledge. This seems to be a blatant violation of some sort of noncircularity condition; but it is the way we talk. It therefore would seem that a picture which suggests this condition must be the wrong picture.

Suppose most of the φ's are in fact satisfied by a unique object. Is that object necessarily the referent of '*X*' for *A*? Let's suppose someone says that Gödel is the man who proved the incompleteness of arithmetic, and this man is suitably well educated and is even able to give an independent account of the incompleteness theorem. He doesn't just say, 'Well, that's Gödel's theorem', or whatever. He actually states a certain theorem, which he attributes to Gödel as the discoverer. Is it the case, then, that if most of the φ's are satisfied by a unique object *y*, then *y* is the referent of the name '*X*' for *A*? Let's take a simple case. In the case of Gödel that's practically the only thing many people have heard about him—that he discovered the incompleteness of arithmetic. Does it follow that whoever discovered the incompleteness of arithmetic is the referent of 'Gödel'?

Imagine the following blatantly fictional situation. (I hope Professor Gödel is not present.) Suppose that Gödel was not in fact the author of this theorem. A man named 'Schmidt', whose body was found in Vienna under mysterious circumstances many years ago, actually did the work in question. His friend Gödel somehow got hold of the manuscript and it was thereafter attributed to Gödel. On the view in question, then, when our ordinary man uses the name 'Gödel', he really means to refer to Schmidt, because Schmidt is the unique person satisfying the description, 'the man who discovered the incompleteness of arithmetic'. Of course you might try changing it to 'the man who *published* the discovery of the incompleteness of arithmetic'. By changing the story a little further one can make even this formulation false. Anyway, most people might not even know whether the thing was published or got around by word of mouth. Let's stick to 'the man who discovered the incompleteness of arithmetic'. So, since the man who discovered the incompleteness of arithmetic is in fact Schmidt, we, when we talk about 'Gödel', are in fact always referring to Schmidt. But it seems to me that we are not. We simply are not. One reply, which I will discuss later, might be: You should say instead, 'the man to whom the incompleteness of arithmetic is commonly attributed', or something like that. Let's see what we can do with that later.

But it may seem to many of you that this is a very odd example, or that such a situation occurs rarely. This also is a tribute to the education of philosophers. Very often we use a name on the basis of considerable misinformation. The case of mathematics used in the fictive example is a good case in point. What do we know about Peano? What many people in this room may 'know' about Peano is that he was the discoverer of certain axioms which characterize the sequence of natural numbers, the so-called 'Peano axioms'. Probably some people can even state them. I have been told that these axioms were not first discovered by Peano but by Dedekind. Peano was of course not a dishonest man. I am told that his footnotes include a credit to Dedekind. Somehow the footnote has been ignored. So on the theory in question the term 'Peano', as we use it, really refers to—now that you've heard it you see that you were really all the time talking about—Dedekind. But you were not. Such illustrations could be multiplied indefinitely.

Even worse misconceptions, of course, occur to the layman. In a previous example I supposed people to identify Einstein by reference to his work on relativity. Actually, I often used to hear that Einstein's most famous achievement was the invention of the atomic bomb. So when we refer to Einstein, we refer to the inventor of the atomic bomb. But this is not so. Columbus was the first man to realize that the earth was round. He was also the first European to land in the western hemisphere. Probably none of these things are true, and therefore, when people use the term 'Columbus' they really refer to some Greek if they use the roundness of the earth, or to some Norseman, perhaps, if they use the 'discovery of America'. But they don't. So it does not seem that if most of the $\varphi$'s are satisfied by a unique object $y$, then $y$ is the referent of the name. This seems simply to be false.[36]

[36] The cluster-of-descriptions theory of naming would make 'Peano discovered the axioms for number theory' express a trivial truth, not a misconception, and similarly for other misconceptions about the history of science. Some who have conceded such cases to me have argued that there are *other* uses of the same proper names satisfying the cluster theory. For example, it is argued, if we say, 'Gödel proved the incompleteness of arithmetic,' we are, of course, referring to Gödel, not to Schmidt. But, if we say, 'Gödel relied on a diagonal argument in this step of the proof,' don't we here, perhaps, refer to *whoever proved the theorem*? Similarly, if someone asks, 'What did Aristotle (or Shakespeare) have in mind here?', isn't he talking about the author of the passage in question, whoever he is? By analogy to Donnellan's usage for descriptions, this might be called an "attributive' use of proper names. If this is so, then assuming the Gödel-Schmidt story, the sentence 'Gödel proved the incompleteness theorem' is false, but 'Gödel used a diagonal argument in the proof' is (at least in some contexts) true, and the reference of the name 'Gödel' is ambiguous. Since some counterexamples remain, the

Thesis (4): If the vote yields no unique object the name does not refer. Really this case has been covered before—has been covered in my previous examples. First, the vote may not yield a *unique* object, as in the case of Cicero or Feynman. Secondly, suppose it yields *no* object, that nothing satisfies most, or even any, substantial number, of the φ's. Does that mean the name doesn't refer? No: in the same way that you may have false beliefs about a person which may actually be true of someone else, so you may have false beliefs which are true of absolutely no one. And these may constitute the totality of your beliefs. Suppose, to vary the example about Gödel, no one had discovered the incompleteness of arithmetic—perhaps the proof simply materialized by a random scattering of atoms on a piece of paper—the man Gödel being lucky enough to have been present when this improbable event occurred. Further, suppose arithmetic is in fact complete. One wouldn't really expect a random scattering of atoms to produce a correct proof. A subtle error, unknown through the decades, has still been unnoticed—or perhaps not actually unnoticed, but the friends of Gödel. . . . So even if the conditions are not satisfied

---

cluster-of-descriptions theory would still, in general, be false, which was my main point in the text; but it would be applicable in a wider class of cases than I thought. I think, however, that no such ambiguity need be postulated. It is, perhaps, true that sometimes when someone uses the name 'Gödel', his main interest is in whoever proved the theorem, and *perhaps*, in some sense, he 'refers' to him. I do not think that this case is different from the case of Smith and Jones in n. 3, p. 25. If I mistake Jones for Smith, I may *refer* (in an appropriate sense) to Jones when I say that Smith is raking the leaves; nevertheless I do not use 'Smith' ambiguously, as a name sometimes of Smith and sometimes of Jones, but univocally as a name of Smith. Similarly, if I erroneously think that Aristotle wrote such-and-such passage, I may perhaps sometimes use 'Aristotle' to *refer* to the actual author of the passage, even though there is no ambiguity in my use of the name. In both cases, I will withdraw my original statement, and my original use of the name, if apprised of the facts. Recall that, in these lectures, 'referent' is used in the technical sense of the thing named by a name (or uniquely satisfying a description), and there should be no confusion.

by a unique object the name may still refer. I gave you the case of Jonah last week. Biblical scholars, as I said, think that Jonah really existed. It isn't because they think that someone ever was swallowed by a big fish or even went to Nineveh to preach. These conditions may be true of no one whatsoever and yet the name 'Jonah' really has a referent. In the case above of Einstein's invention of the bomb, possibly no one really deserves to be called the 'inventor' of the device.

Thesis 5 says that the statement 'If $X$ exists, then $X$ has most of the $\varphi$'s', is *a priori* true for $A$. Notice that even in a case where (3) and (4) *happen* to be true, a typical speaker hardly knows *a priori* that they are, as required by the theory. I *think* that my belief about Gödel *is* in fact correct and that the 'Schmidt' story is just a fantasy. But the belief hardly constitutes *a priori* knowledge.

What's going on here? Can we rescue the theory?[37] First, one may try and vary these descriptions—not think of the famous achievements of a man but, let's say, of something else, and try and use that as our description. Maybe by enough futzing around someone might eventually get something out

[37] It has been suggested to me that someone might argue that a name is associated with a 'referential' use of a description in Donnellan's sense. For example, although we identify Gödel as the author of the incompleteness theorem, we are talking about him even if he turns out not to have proved the theorem. Theses (2)–(6) could then fail; but nevertheless each name would abbreviate a description, though the role of description in naming would differ radically from that imagined by Frege and Russell. As I have said above, I am inclined to reject Donnellan's formulation of the notion of referential definite description. Even if Donnellan's analysis is accepted, however, it is clear that the present proposal should not be. For a referential definite description, such as 'the man drinking champagne', is typically withdrawn when the speaker realizes that it does not apply to its object. If a Gödelian fraud were exposed, Gödel would no longer be called 'the author of the incompleteness theorem' but he would still be called 'Gödel'. The name, therefore, does not abbreviate the description.

of this;[38] however, most of the attempts that one tries are open to counterexamples or other objections. Let me give an example of this. In the case of Gödel one may say, 'Well, "Gödel" doesn't mean "the man who proved the incompleteness of arithmetic" '. Look, all we really know is that most people *think* that Gödel proved the incompleteness of arithmetic, that Gödel is the man to whom the incompleteness of arithmetic is commonly attributed. So when I determine the referent of the name 'Gödel', I don't say to myself, 'by "Gödel" I shall mean "the man who proved the incompleteness of arithmetic, whoever he is" '. That might turn out to be Schmidt or Post. But instead I shall mean 'the man who most people *think* proved the incompleteness of arithmetic'.

Is this right? First, it seems to me that it's open to counterexamples of the same type as I gave before, though the counterexamples may be more recherché. Suppose, in the case of Peano mentioned previously, unbeknownst to the speaker, most people (at least by now) thoroughly realize that the number-theoretic axioms should not be attributed to him. Most people don't credit them to Peano but now correctly ascribe them to Dedekind. So then even the man to whom this thing is commonly attributed will still be Dedekind and not Peano. Still, the speaker, having picked up the old outmoded

[38] As Robert Nozick pointed out to me, there is a sense in which a description theory must be trivially true if any theory of the reference of names, spelled out in terms independent of the notion of reference, is available. For if such a theory gives conditions under which an object is to be the referent of a name, then it of course uniquely satisfies these conditions. Since I am not pretending to give any theory which eliminates the notion of reference in this sense, I am not aware of any such trivial fulfillment of the description theory and doubt that one exists. (A description using the notion of the reference of a name is easily available but circular, as we saw in our discussion of Kneale.) If any such trivial fulfillment were available, however, the arguments I have given show that the description must be one of a completely different sort from that supposed by Frege, Russell, Searle, Strawson and other advocates of the description theory.

belief, may still be referring to Peano, and hold a false belief about Peano, not a true belief about Dedekind.

But second, and perhaps more significantly, such a criterion violates the noncircularity condition. How is this? It is true that most of us think that Gödel proved the incompleteness of arithmetic. Why is this so? We certainly say, and sincerely, 'Gödel proved the incompleteness of arithmetic'. Does it follow from that that we believe that Gödel proved the incompleteness of arithmetic—that we attribute the incompleteness of arithmetic to this man? No. Not just from that. We have to be *referring to Gödel* when we say 'Gödel proved the incompleteness of arithmetic'. If, in fact, we were always referring to Schmidt, then we would be attributing the incompleteness of arithmetic to Schmidt and not to Gödel—if we used the sound 'Gödel' as the name of the man whom I am calling 'Schmidt'.

But we do in fact refer to Gödel. How do we do this? Well, not by saying to ourselves, 'By "Gödel" I shall mean the man to whom the incompleteness of arithmetic is commonly attributed'. If we did that we would run into a circle. Here we are all in this room. Actually in this institution[39] some people have met the man, but in many institutions this is not so. All of us in the community are trying to determine the reference by saying 'Gödel is to be the man to whom the incompleteness of arithmetic is commonly attributed'. None of us will get started with any attribution unless there is some independent criterion for the reference of the name other than 'the man to whom the incompleteness of arithmetic is commonly attributed'. Otherwise all we will be saying is, 'We attribute this achievement to the man to whom we attribute it', without saying who that man is, without giving any independent criterion of the reference, and so the determination will be circular. This then is a violation of the condition I have

[39] Princeton University.

marked '*C*', and cannot be used in any theory of reference.

Of course you might try to avoid circularity by passing the buck. This is mentioned by Strawson, who says in his footnote on these matters that one man's reference may derive from another's.

> The identifying description, though it must not include a reference to the speaker's own reference to the particular in question, may include a reference to another's reference to that particular. If a putatively identifying description is of this latter kind, then, indeed, the question, whether it is a genuinely identifying description, turns on the question, whether the reference it refers to is itself a genuinely identifying reference. So one reference may borrow its credentials, as a genuinely identifying reference, from another; and that from another. But this regress is not infinite.[40]

I may then say, 'Look, by "Gödel" I shall mean the man Joe thinks proved the incompleteness of arithmetic'. Joe may then pass the thing over to Harry. One has to be very careful that this doesn't come round in a circle. Is one really sure that this won't happen? If you could be sure yourself of knowing such a chain, and that everyone else in the chain is using the proper conditions and so is not getting out of it, then maybe you could get back to the man by referring to such a chain in that way, borrowing the references one by one. However, although in general such chains do exist for a living man, you won't know what the chain is. You won't be sure what descriptions the other man is using, so the thing won't go into a circle, or whether by appealing to Joe you won't get back to the right man at all. So you cannot use this as your identifying description with any confidence. You may not even remember from whom you heard of Gödel.

What is the true picture of what's going on? Maybe reference doesn't really take place at all! After all, we don't really know

[40] Strawson, op. cit., p. 182 n.

that any of the properties we use to identify the man are right. We don't know that they pick out a unique object. So what *does* make my use of 'Cicero' into a name of *him*? The picture which leads to the cluster-of-descriptions theory is something like this: One is isolated in a room; the entire community of other speakers, everything else, could disappear; and one determines the reference for himself by saying—'By "Gödel" I shall mean the man, whoever he is, who proved the incompleteness of arithmetic'. Now you can do this if you want to. There's nothing really preventing it. You can just stick to that determination. If that's what you do, then if Schmidt discovered the incompleteness of arithmetic you *do* refer to him when you say 'Gödel did such and such'.

But that's not what most of us do. Someone, let's say, a baby, is born; his parents call him by a certain name. They talk about him to their friends. Other people meet him. Through various sorts of talk the name is spread from link to link as if by a chain. A speaker who is on the far end of this chain, who has heard about, say Richard Feynman, in the market place or elsewhere, may be referring to Richard Feynman even though he can't remember from whom he first heard of Feynman or from whom he ever heard of Feynman. He knows that Feynman is a famous physicist. A certain passage of communication reaching ultimately to the man himself does reach the speaker. He then is referring to Feynman even though he can't identify him uniquely. He doesn't know what a Feynman diagram is, he doesn't know what the Feynman theory of pair production and annihilation is. Not only that: he'd have trouble distinguishing between Gell-Mann and Feynman. So he doesn't have to know these things, but, instead, a chain of communication going back to Feynman himself has been established, by virtue of his membership in a community which passed the name on from link to link, not by a ceremony that he makes in private in his study: 'By "Feynman" I shall mean the man who did such and such and such and such'.

How does this view differ from Strawson's suggestion, mentioned before, that one identifying reference may borrow its credentials from another? Certainly Strawson had a good insight in the passage quoted; on the other hand, he certainly shows a difference at least in emphasis from the picture I advocate, since he confines the remark to a footnote. The main text advocates the cluster-of-descriptions theory. Just because Strawson makes his remark in the context of a description theory, his view therefore differs from mine in one important respect. Strawson apparently requires that the speaker must *know* from whom he got his reference, so that he can say: 'By "Gödel" I mean the man *Jones* calls "Gödel" '. If he does not remember how he picked up the reference, he cannot give such a description. The present theory sets no such requirement. As I said, I may well not remember from whom I heard of Gödel, and I may think I remember from which people I heard the name, but wrongly.

These considerations show that the view advocated here can lead to consequences which actually *diverge* from those of Strawson's footnote. Suppose that the speaker has heard the name 'Cicero' from Smith and others, who use the name to refer to a famous Roman orator. He later thinks, however, that he picked up the name from Jones, who (unknown to the speaker) uses 'Cicero' as the name of a notorious German spy and has never heard of any orators of the ancient world. Then, according to Strawson's paradigm, the speaker must determine his reference by the resolution, 'I shall use "Cicero" to refer to the man whom Jones calls by that name', while on the present view, the referent will be the orator in spite of the speaker's false impression about where he picked up the name. The point is that Strawson, trying to fit the chain of communication view into the description theory, relies on what the speaker *thinks* was the source of his reference. If the speaker has forgotten his source, the description Strawson uses is unavailable to him; if he misremembers it, Strawson's paradigm can give the wrong results. On our view, it is not how the speaker thinks he got the reference, but the actual chain of communication, which is relevant.

I think I said the other time that philosophical theories are in danger of being false, and so I wasn't going to present an alternative theory. Have I just done so? Well, in a way; but my characterization has been far less specific than a real set of necessary and sufficient conditions for reference would be. Obviously the name is passed on from link to link. But of course not every sort of causal chain reaching from me to a certain man will do for me to make a reference. There may be a causal chain from our use of the term 'Santa Claus' to a certain historical saint, but still the children, when they use this, by this time probably do not refer to that saint. So other conditions must be satisfied in order to make this into a really rigorous theory of reference. I don't know that I'm going to do this because, first, I'm sort of too lazy at the moment; secondly, rather than giving a set of necessary and sufficient conditions which will work for a term like reference, I want to present just a *better picture* than the picture presented by the received views.

Haven't I been very unfair to the description theory? Here I have stated it very precisely—more precisely, perhaps, than it has been stated by any of its advocates. So then it's easy to refute. Maybe if I tried to state mine with sufficient precision in the form of six or seven or eight theses, it would also turn out that when you examine the theses one by one, they will all be false. That might even be so, but the difference is this. What I think the examples I've given show is not simply that there's some technical error here or some mistake there, but that the whole picture given by this theory of how reference is determined seems to be wrong from the fundamentals. It seems to be wrong to think that we give ourselves some properties which somehow qualitatively uniquely pick out an object and determine our reference in that manner. What I am trying to present is a better picture—a picture which, if more details were to be filled in, might be refined so as to give more exact conditions for reference to take place.

One might never reach a set of necessary and sufficient conditions. I don't know, I'm always sympathetic to Bishop Butler's 'Everything is what it is and not another thing'—in the nontrivial sense that philosophical analyses of some concept like reference, in completely different terms which make no mention of reference, are very apt to fail. Of course in any particular case when one is given an analysis one has to look at it and see whether it is true or false. One can't just cite this maxim to oneself and then turn the page. But more cautiously, I want to present a better picture without giving a set of necessary and sufficient conditions for reference. Such conditions would be very complicated, but what is true is that it's in virtue of our connection with other speakers in the community, going back to the referent himself, that we refer to a certain man.

There may be some cases where the description picture is true, where some man really gives a name by going into the privacy of his room and saying that the referent is to be the unique thing with certain identifying properties. 'Jack the Ripper' was a possible example which I gave. Another was 'Hesperus'. Yet another case which can be forced into this description is that of meeting someone and being told his name. Except for a belief in the description theory, in its importance in other cases, one probably wouldn't think that that was a case of giving oneself a description, i.e., 'the guy I'm just meeting now'. But one can put it in these terms if one wishes, and if one has never heard the name in any other way. Of course, if you're introduced to a man and told, 'That's

Einstein', you've heard of him before, it may be wrong, and so on. But maybe in some cases such a paradigm works—especially for the man who first gives someone or something a name. Or he points to a star and says, 'That is to be Alpha Centauri'. So he can really make himself this ceremony: 'By "Alpha Centauri" I shall mean the star right over there with such and such coordinates'. But in general this picture fails. In general our reference depends not just on what we think ourselves, but on other people in the community, the history of how the name reached one, and things like that. It is by following such a history that one gets to the reference.

More exact conditions are very complicated to give. They seem in a way somehow different in the case of a famous man and one who isn't so famous. For example, a teacher tells his class that Newton was famous for being the first man to think there's a force pulling things to the earth; I think that's what little kids think Newton's greatest achievement was. I won't say what the merits of such an achievement would be, but, anyway, we may suppose that just being told that this was the sole content of Newton's discovery gives the students a false belief *about Newton*, even though they have never heard of him before. If, on the other hand,[41] the teacher uses the name 'George Smith'—a man by that name is actually his next door neighbor—and says that George Smith first squared the circle, does it follow from this that the students have a false belief about the teacher's neighbor? The teacher doesn't tell them that Smith is his neighbor, nor does he believe Smith first squared the circle. He isn't particularly trying to get any belief *about the neighbor* into the students' heads. He tries to inculcate the belief that there was a man who squared the circle, but not a belief about any particular man—he just pulls out the first name that occurs to him—as it happens, he uses his neighbor's name. It doesn't seem clear in that case that the

[41] The essential points of this example were suggested by Richard Miller.

students have a false belief about the neighbor, even though there is a causal chain going back to the neighbor. I am not sure about this. At any rate more refinements need to be added to make this even begin to be a set of necessary and sufficient conditions. In that sense it's not a theory, but is supposed to give a better picture of what is actually going on.

A rough statement of a theory might be the following: An initial 'baptism' takes place. Here the object may be named by ostension, or the reference of the name may be fixed by a description.[42] When the name is 'passed from link to link', the receiver of the name must, I think, intend when he learns it to use it with the same reference as the man from whom he heard it. If I hear the name 'Napoleon' and decide it would be a nice name for my pet aardvark, I do not satisfy this condition.[43] (Perhaps it is some such failure to keep the reference

[42] A good example of a baptism whose reference was fixed by means of a description was that of naming Neptune in n. 33, p. 79. The case of a baptism by ostension can perhaps be subsumed under the description concept also. Thus the primary applicability of the description theory is to cases of initial baptism. Descriptions are also used to fix a reference in cases of designation which are similar to naming except that the terms introduced are not usually called 'names'. The terms 'one meter', '100 degrees Centigrade', have already been given as examples, and other examples will be given later in these lectures. Two things should be emphasized concerning the case of introducing a name via a description in an initial baptism. First, the description used is not synonymous with the name it introduces but rather fixes its reference. Here we differ from the usual description theorists. Second, most cases of initial baptism are far from those which originally inspired the description theory. Usually a baptizer is acquainted in some sense with the object he names and is able to name it ostensively. Now the inspiration of the description theory lay in the fact that we can often use names of famous figures of the past who are long dead and with whom no living person is acquainted; and it is precisely these cases which, on our view, cannot be correctly explained by a description theory.

[43] I can transmit the name of the aardvark to other people. For each of these people, as for me, there will be a certain sort of causal or historical connection between my use of the name and the Emperor of the French, but not one of the required type.

fixed which accounts for the divergence of present uses of 'Santa Claus' from the alleged original use.)

Notice that the preceding outline hardly *eliminates* the notion of reference; on the contrary, it takes the notion of intending to use the same reference as a given. There is also an appeal to an initial baptism which is explained in terms either of fixing a reference by a description, or ostension (if ostension is not to be subsumed under the other category).[44] (Perhaps there are other possibilities for initial baptisms.) Further, the George Smith case casts some doubt as to the sufficiency of the conditions. Even if the teacher does refer to his neighbor, is it clear that he has passed on his reference to the pupils? Why shouldn't their belief be about any other man named 'George Smith'? If he says that Newton was hit by an apple, somehow his task of transmitting a reference is easier, since he has communicated a common misconception about Newton.

To repeat, I may not have presented a theory, but I do think that I have presented a better picture than that given by description theorists.

I think the next topic I shall want to talk about is that of statements of identity. Are these necessary or contingent? The matter has been in some dispute in recent philosophy. First,

[44] Once we realize that the description used to fix the reference of a name is not synonymous with it, then the description theory can be regarded as presupposing the notion of naming or reference. The requirement I made that the description used not itself involve the notion of reference in a circular way is something else and is crucial if the description theory is to have any value at all. The reason is that the description theorist supposes that each speaker essentially uses the description he gives in an initial act of naming to determine his reference. Clearly, if he introduces the name 'Cicero' by the determination, 'By "Cicero" I shall refer to the man I call "Cicero",' he has by this ceremony determined no reference at all.

Not all description theorists thought that they were eliminating the notion of reference altogether. Perhaps some realized that some notion of ostension, or primitive reference, is required to back it up. Certainly Russell did.

everyone agrees that descriptions can be used to make contingent identity statements. If it is true that the man who invented bifocals was the first Postmaster General of the United States—that these were one and the same—it's contingently true. That is, it might have been the case that one man invented bifocals and another was the first Postmaster General of the United States. So certainly when you make identity statements using descriptions—when you say 'the $x$ such that $\varphi x$ and the $x$ such that $\psi x$ are one and the same'—that can be a contingent fact. But philosophers have been interested also in the question of identity statements between names. When we say 'Hesperus is Phosphorus' or 'Cicero is Tully', is what we are saying necessary or contingent? Further, they've been interested in another type of identity statement, which comes from scientific theory. We identify, for example, light with electromagnetic radiation between certain limits of wavelengths, or with a stream of photons. We identify heat with the motion of molecules; sound with a certain sort of wave disturbance in the air; and so on. Concerning such statements the following thesis is commonly held. First, that these are obviously contingent identities: we've found out that light is a stream of photons, but of course it might not have been a stream of photons. Heat is in fact the motion of molecules; we found that out, but heat might not have been the motion of molecules. Secondly, many philosophers feel damned lucky that these examples are around. Now, why? These philosophers, whose views are expounded in a vast literature, hold to a thesis called 'the identity thesis' with respect to some psychological concepts. They think, say, that pain is just a certain material state of the brain or of the body, or what have you—say the stimulation of C-fibers. (It doesn't matter what.) Some people have then objected, 'Well, look, there's perhaps a *correlation* between pain and these states of the body; but this must just be a contingent correlation between two different things, because it was an empirical discovery that this correlation ever held. Therefore, by "pain" we must mean something different from this state of the body or brain; and, therefore, they must be two different things.'

Then it's said, 'Ah, but you see, this is wrong! Everyone knows that there can be contingent identities.' First, as in the bifocals and Postmaster General case, which I have mentioned before. Second, in the case, believed closer to the present paradigm, of theoretical identifications, such as light and a stream of photons, or water and a certain compound of hydrogen and oxygen. These are all contingent identities. They might have been false. It's no surprise, therefore, that it can be true as a matter of contingent fact and not of any necessity that feeling pain, or seeing red, is just a certain state of the human body. Such psychophysical identifications can be contingent facts just as the other identities are contingent facts. And of course there are widespread motivations—ideological, or just not wanting to have the 'nomological dangler' of mysterious connections not accounted for by the laws of physics, one to one correlations between two different kinds of thing, material states, and things of an entirely different kind, which lead people to want to believe this thesis.

I guess the main thing I'll talk about first is identity statements between names. But I hold the following about the general case. First, that characteristic theoretical identifications like 'Heat is the motion of molecules', are not contingent truths but necessary truths, and here of course I don't mean just physically necessary, but necessary in the highest degree—whatever that means. (Physical necessity, *might* turn out to be necessity in the highest degree. But that's a question which I don't wish to prejudge. At least for this sort of example, it might be that when something's physically necessary, it always is necessary *tout court*.) Second, that the way in which these have turned out to be necessary truths does not seem to me to be a way in which the mind-brain identities could turn out to be either necessary or contingently true. So this analogy has to go. It's hard to see what to put in its place. It's hard to see therefore how to avoid concluding that the two are actually different.

Let me go back to the more mundane case about proper names. This is already mysterious enough. There's a dispute about this between Quine and Ruth Barcan Marcus.[45] Marcus says that identities between names are necessary. If someone thinks that Cicero is Tully, and really uses 'Cicero' and 'Tully' as names, he is thereby committed to holding that his belief is a necessary truth. She uses the term 'mere tag'. Quine replies as follows, 'We may tag the planet Venus, some fine evening, with the proper name "Hesperus". We may tag the same planet again, some day before sunrise, with the proper name "Phosphorus". When we discover that we have tagged the same planet twice our discovery is empirical. And not because the proper names were descriptions.'[46] First, as Quine says when we discovered that we tagged the same planet twice, our discovery was empirical. Another example I think Quine gives in another book is that the same mountain seen from Nepal and from Tibet, or something like that, is from one angle called 'Mt. Everest' (you've heard of that); from another it's supposed to be called 'Gaurisanker'. It can actually be an empirical discovery that Gaurisanker is Everest. (Quine says that the example is actually false. He got the example from Erwin Schrödinger. You wouldn't think the inventor of wave mechanics got things that wrong. I don't know where the mistake is supposed to come from. One could certainly imagine this situation as having been the case; and it's another

[45] Ruth Barcan Marcus, 'Modalities and Intensional Languages' (comments by W. V. Quine, plus discussion) *Boston Studies in the Philosophy of Science*, volume I, Reidel, Dordrecht, Holland, 1963, pp. 77–116.

[46] p. 101.

good illustration of the sort of thing that Quine has in mind.)

What about it? I wanted to find a good quote on the other side from Marcus in this book but I am having trouble locating one. Being present at that discussion, I remember[47] that she advocated the view that if you really have names, a good dictionary should be able to tell you whether they have the same reference. So someone should be able, by looking in the dictionary, to say that Hesperus and Phosphorus are the same. Now this does not seem to be true. It does seem, to many people, to be a consequence of the view that identities between names are necessary. Therefore the view that identity statements between names are necessary has usually been rejected. Russell's conclusion was somewhat different. He did think there should never be any empirical question whether two names have the same reference. This isn't satisfied for ordinary names, but it is satisfied when you're naming your own sense datum, or something like that. You say, 'Here, this, and that (designating the same sense datum by both demonstratives).' So you can tell without empirical investigation that you're naming the same thing twice; the conditions are satisfied. Since this won't apply to ordinary cases of naming, ordinary 'names' cannot be genuine names.

What should we think about this? First, it's true that someone can use the name 'Cicero' to refer to Cicero and the name 'Tully' to refer to Cicero also, and not know that Cicero is Tully. So it seems that we do not necessarily know *a priori* that an identity statement between names is true. It doesn't follow from this that the statement so expressed is a contingent one if true. This is what I've emphasized in my first lecture. There is a very strong feeling that leads one to think that, if you can't know something by *a priori* ratiocination, then it's got to be contingent: it might have turned out otherwise; but nevertheless I think this feeling is wrong.

[47] p. 115.

Let's suppose we refer to the same heavenly body twice, as 'Hesperus' and 'Phosphorus'. We say: Hesperus is that star over there in the evening; Phosphorus is that star over there in the morning. Actually, Hesperus is Phosphorus. Are there really circumstances under which Hesperus wouldn't have been Phosphorus? Supposing that Hesperus is Phosphorus, let's try to describe a possible situation in which it would not have been. Well, it's easy. Someone goes by and he calls two *different* stars 'Hesperus' and 'Phosphorus'. It may even be under the same conditions as prevailed when we introduced the names 'Hesperus' and 'Phosphorus'. But are those circumstances in which Hesperus is not Phosphorus or would not have been Phosphorus? It seems to me that they are not.

Now, of course I'm committed to saying that they're not, by saying that such terms as 'Hesperus' and 'Phosphorus', when used as names, are rigid designators. They refer in every possible world to the planet Venus. Therefore, in that possible world too, the planet Venus is the planet Venus and it doesn't matter what any other person has said in this other possible world. How should *we* describe this situation? He can't have pointed to Venus twice, and in the one case called it 'Hesperus' and in the other 'Phosphorus', as we did. If he did so, then 'Hesperus is Phosphorus' would have been true in that situation too. He pointed maybe neither time to the planet Venus—at least one time he didn't point to the planet Venus, let's say when he pointed to the body he called 'Phosphorus'. Then in that case we can certainly say that the name 'Phosphorus' might not have referred to Phosphorus. We can even say that in the very position when viewed in the morning that we found Phosphorus, it might have been the case that Phosphorus was not there—that something else was there, and that even, under certain circumstances it would have been *called* 'Phosphorus'. But that still is not a case in which Phosphorus was not Hesperus. There might be a possible world in which, a possible counterfactual situation in which, 'Hesperus' and 'Phosphorus' weren't names of the things they in fact are names of. Someone, if he did determine their reference by identifying descriptions, might even have used the very identifying descriptions we used. But still that's not a case in which Hesperus wasn't Phosphorus. For there couldn't have been such a case, given that Hesperus is Phosphorus.

Now this seems very strange because in advance, we are inclined to say, the answer to the question whether Hesperus is Phosphorus might have turned out either way. So aren't there really two possible worlds—one in which Hesperus was Phosphorus, the other in which Hesperus wasn't Phosphorus—in advance of our discovering that these were the same? First, there's one sense in which things might turn out either way, in which it's clear that that doesn't imply that the way it finally turns out isn't necessary. For example, the four color theorem might turn out to be true and might turn out to be false. It might turn out either way. It still doesn't mean that the way it turns out is not necessary. Obviously, the 'might' here is purely 'epistemic'—it merely expresses our present state of ignorance, or uncertainty.

But it seems that in the Hesperus-Phosphorus case, something even stronger is true. The evidence I have before I know that Hesperus is Phosphorus is that I see a certain star or a certain heavenly body in the evening and call it 'Hesperus', and in the morning and call it 'Phosphorus'. I know these things. There certainly is a possible world in which a man should have seen a certain star at a certain position in the evening and called it 'Hesperus' and a certain star in the morning and called it 'Phosphorus'; and should have concluded—should have found out by empirical investigation—that he names two different stars, or two different heavenly bodies. At least one of these stars or heavenly bodies was not Phosphorus, otherwise it couldn't have come out that way. But that's true. And so it's true that given the evidence that someone has antecedent to his empirical investigation, he can be placed in a sense in exactly the same situation, that is a qualitatively identical epistemic situation, and call two heavenly bodies 'Hesperus' and 'Phosphorus', without their being identical. So in that sense we can say that it might have turned out either way. Not that it might have turned out either way as to Hesperus's being Phosphorus. Though for all we knew in advance, Hesperus wasn't Phosphorus, that couldn't have turned out any other way, in a sense. But being put in a situation where we have exactly the same evidence, qualitatively speaking, it could have turned out that Hesperus was not Phosphorus; that is, in a counterfactual world in which 'Hesperus' and 'Phosphorus' were not used in the way that we use them, as names of this planet, but as names of some other objects, one could have had qualitatively identical evidence and concluded that 'Hesperus' and 'Phosphorus' named two different objects.[48] But we, using the names as we do right now, can say in advance, that if Hesperus and Phosphorus are one and the same, then in no other possible world can they be different. We use 'Hesperus' as the name of a certain body and 'Phosphorus' as the name of a certain body. We use them as names of those bodies in all possible worlds. If, in fact, they are the *same* body, then in any other possible world we have to use them as a name of that object. And so in any other possible world it will be true that Hesperus is Phosphorus. So two things are true: first, that we do not know *a priori* that Hesperus is Phosphorus, and are in no position to find out the answer except empirically. Second, this is so because we could have evidence qualitatively indistinguishable from the evidence we have and determine the reference of the two names by the positions of two planets in the sky, without the planets being the same.

[48] There is a more elaborate discussion of this point in the third lecture, where its relation to a certain sort of counterpart theory is also mentioned.

Of course, it is only a contingent truth (not true in every other possible world) that the star seen over there in the evening is the star seen over there in the morning, because there are possible worlds in which Phosphorus was not visible in the morning. But that contingent truth shouldn't be identified with the statement that Hesperus is Phosphorus. It could only be so identified if you thought that it was a necessary truth that Hesperus is visible over there in the evening or that Phosphorus is visible over there in the morning. But neither of those are necessary truths even if that's the way we pick out the planet. These are the contingent marks by which we identify a certain planet and give it a name.

# LECTURE III: JANUARY 29, 1970

What's been accomplished, if anything, up to now? First, I've argued that a popular view about how names get their reference in general doesn't apply. It is in general not the case that the reference of a name is determined by some uniquely identifying marks, some unique properties satisfied by the referent and known or believed to be true of that referent by the speaker. First, the properties believed by the speaker need not be uniquely specifying. Second, even in the case where they are, they may not be uniquely true of the actual referent of the speaker's use but of something else or of nothing. This is the case where the speaker has erroneous beliefs about some person. He does not have correct beliefs about another person, but erroneous beliefs about a certain person. In these cases the reference actually seems to be determined by the fact that the speaker is a member of a community of speakers who use the name. The name has been passed to him by tradition from link to link.

Second, I've argued, even if in some special cases, notably some cases of initial baptism, a referent *is* determined by a description, by some uniquely identifying property, what that property is doing in many cases of designation is not giving a synonym, giving something for which the name is an abbreviation; it is, rather, fixing a reference. It fixes the reference by some contingent marks of the object. The name denoting that object is then used to refer to that object, even in referring to counterfactual situations where the object doesn't have the properties in question. An example was the case of a meter.

Finally, at the end of the talk last time we were talking about statements of identity. Statements of identity should seem very simple but they are somehow very puzzling to philosophers. I cannot be sure in my own case whether I have all the possible confusions that can be generated by this relation straightened out. Some philosophers have found the relation so confusing that they change it. It is, for example, thought that if you have two names like 'Cicero' and 'Tully' and say that Cicero is Tully, you can't really be saying of the object which is both Cicero and Tully that it is identical with itself. On the contrary, 'Cicero is Tully' can express an empirical discovery, as we mentioned before. And so some philosophers, even Frege at one early stage of his writing, have taken identity to be a relation between names. Identity, so they say, is not the relation between an object and itself, but is the relation which holds between two names when they designate the same object.

This occurs even in the more recent literature. I didn't bring the book along, but J. B. Rosser, the distinguished logician, writes in his book, *Logic for Mathematicians*,[49] that we say that $x = y$ if and only if '$x$' and '$y$' are names for the same object. He remarks that the corresponding statement about the object itself, that it in no way differs from itself, is of course trivial; and so, presumably, cannot be what we mean. This is an especially unusual paradigm of what the identity relationship should be because it would apply very rarely. As far as I know, outside the militant black nationalist movement no one has ever been named '$x$'. Seriously speaking, of course, '$x$' and '$y$' in the open sentence '$x = y$' are not names at all, they are variables. And they can occur with identity as bound variables in a closed sentence. If you say for every $x$ and $y$, if $x = y$ then

[49] New York, McGraw-Hill (1953), see Chapter VII, 'Equality'.

$y = x$, or something like that—no names occur in that statement at all, nor is anything said about names. This statement would be true even though the human race had never existed or, though it did exist, never produced the phenomenon of names.

If anyone ever inclines to this particular account of identity, let's suppose we *gave* him his account. Suppose identity *were* a relation in English between the names. I shall introduce an artificial relation called 'schmidentity' (not a word of English) which I now stipulate to hold only between an object and itself.[50] Now then the question whether Cicero is schmidentical with Tully can arise, and if it does arise the same problems will hold for this statement as were thought in the case of the original identity statement to give the belief that this was a relation between the names. If anyone thinks about this seriously, I think he will see that therefore probably his original account of identity was not necessary, and probably not possible, for the problems it was originally meant to solve, and that therefore it should be dropped, and identity should just be taken to be the relation between a thing and itself. This sort of device can be used for a number of philosophical problems.

We have concluded that an identity statement between names, when true at all, is necessarily true, even though one may not know it *a priori*. Suppose we identify Hesperus as a

[50] Of course, the device will fail to convince a philosopher who wants to argue that an artificial language or concept of the supposed type is logically impossible. In the present case, some philosophers have thought that a relation, being essentially two-termed, cannot hold between a thing and itself. This position is plainly absurd. Someone can be his own worst enemy, his own severest critic and the like. Some relations are reflexive such as the relation 'no richer than'. Identity or schmidentity is nothing but the smallest reflexive relation.

I hope to elaborate on the utility of this device of imagining a hypothetical language elsewhere.

certain star seen in the evening and Phosphorus as a certain star, or a certain heavenly body, seen in the morning; then there may be possible worlds in which two different planets would have been seen in just those positions in the evening and morning. However, at least one of them, and maybe both, would not have been Hesperus, and then that would not have been a situation in which Hesperus was not Phosphorus. It might have been a situation in which the planet seen in this position in the evening was not the planet seen in this position in the morning; but that is not a situation in which Hesperus was not Phosphorus. It might also, if people gave the names 'Hesperus' and 'Phosphorus' to these planets, be a situation in which some planet other than Hesperus was called 'Hesperus'. But even so, it would not be a situation in which Hesperus itself was not Phosphorus.[51]

Some of the problems which bother people in these situations, as I have said, come from an identification, or as I would put it, a confusion, between what we can know *a priori* in advance and what is necessary. Certain statements—and the identity statement is a paradigm of such a statement on my view—if true at all must be necessarily true. One does know *a priori*, by philosophical analysis, that *if* such an identity statement is true it is necessarily true.

One qualification: when I say 'Hesperus is Phosphorus' is necessarily true, I of course do not deny that situations might have obtained in which there was no such planet as Venus at all, and therefore no Hesperus and no Phosphorus. In that case, there is a question whether the identity statement 'Hesperus is Phosphorus' would be true, false, or neither true

[51] Recall that we describe the situation in our language, not the language that the people in that situation would have used. Hence we must use the terms 'Hesperus' and 'Phosphorus' with the same reference as in the actual world. The fact that people in that situation might or might not have used these names for different planets is irrelevant. So is the fact that they might have done so using the very same descriptions as we did to fix their references.

nor false.[62] And if we take the last option, is 'Hesperus = Phosphorus' necessary because it is never false, or should we require that a necessary truth be *true* in all possible worlds? I am leaving such problems outside my considerations altogether. If we wish to be somewhat more careful, we could replace the statement 'Hesperus is Phosphorus' by the conditional, 'If Hesperus exists then Hesperus is Phosphorus', cautiously taking only the latter to be necessary. Unfortunately this conditional involves us in the problem of singular attributions of existence, one I cannot discuss here. In particular, philosophers sympathetic to the description theory of naming often argue that one cannot ever say of an object that it exists. A supposed statement about the existence of an object really is, so it's argued, a statement about whether a certain description or property is satisfied. As I have already said, I disagree. Anyway, I can't really go into the problems of existence here.

I want to mention at this point that other considerations about *de re* modality, about an object having essential properties, can only be regarded correctly, in my view, if we recognize the distinction between a prioricity and necessity. One might very well discover essence empirically.

There are some examples of alleged essential properties in an article by Timothy Sprigge.

> The internalist [which means the believer that there are some essential properties] says that the Queen must have been born of royal blood. [He means that *this person* must have been of royal blood.] The anti-essentialist says there would be no contradiction in a news bulletin asserting that it had been established that the Queen was not in fact the child of her supposed parents, but had been secretly adopted by them, and therefore the proposition that she is of royal blood is synthetic . . .

[62] The same three options exist for 'Hesperus is Hesperus', and the answer must be the same as in the case of 'Hesperus is Phosphorus'.

For a time [the anti-essentialist] is winning. Yet there comes a time when his claims appear a trifle too far fetched. The internalist suggests that we cannot imagine that particular we call the Queen having the property of at no stage in her existence being human. If the anti-internalist admits this, admits that it is logically inconceivable that the Queen should have had the property of, say, always being a swan, then he admits that she has at least one internal property. If on the other hand he says that it's only a contingent fact that the Queen has ever been human, he says what it is hard to accept. Can we really consider it as conceivable that she should never have been human?[53]

'At no stage in her existence' and 'always' are justifications Sprigge presumably introduces to allow such possibilities as her right now being changed into a swan—by a wicked witch, I guess. (Or a benign witch.)

One confusion I find in this discussion is that in the first case Sprigge talks about whether there would be any contradiction in supposing that we had an *announcement* that the Queen was born of parents different from the ones she actually had. And in that there is no contradiction. Similarly, though, there is no contradiction in an *announcement* that the Queen, this thing we thought to be a woman, was in fact an angel in human form, or an automaton cleverly constructed by the royal family, who did not want the succession to pass to that bastard so-and-so, or something. Neither of these announcements represent things that we couldn't possibly *discover*, either. What is the question we are asking when we ask whether it's necessary, concerning this woman, that she should either have been of royal blood or have been human? Royal blood is a little complicated, because in order for it to be necessary for her to have been of royal blood it has to be necessary that this particular family line at some time attained to royal power; but the latter fact seems to

[53] 'Internal and External Properties', *Mind* 71 (April, 1962), pp. 202–03.

be contingent. Therefore I suppose it *is* contingent that her blood should ever have been royal.

Let's try and refine the question a little bit. The question really should be, let's say, could the Queen—could this woman herself—have been born of different parents from the parents from whom she actually came? Could she, let's say, have been the daughter instead of Mr. and Mrs. Truman? There would be no contradiction, of course, in an announcement that (I hope the ages do not make this impossible), fantastic as it may sound, she was indeed the daughter of Mr. and Mrs. Truman. I suppose there might even be no contradiction in the discovery that—it seems very suspicious anyway that on either hypothesis she has a sister called Margaret—that these two Margarets were one and the same person flying back and forth in a clever way. At any rate we can imagine discovering all of these things.

But let us suppose that such a discovery is not in fact the case. Let's suppose that the Queen really did come from these parents. Not to go into too many complications here about what a parent is, let's suppose that the parents are the people whose body tissues are sources of the biological sperm and egg. So you get rid of such recherché possibilities as transplants of the sperm from the father, or the egg from the mother, into other bodies, so that in one sense other people might have been her parents. If that happened, in another sense her parents were still the original king and queen. But other than that, can we imagine a situation in which it would have happened that this very woman came out of Mr. and Mrs. Truman? They might have had a child resembling her in many properties. Perhaps in some possible world Mr. and Mrs. Truman even had a child who actually became the Queen of England and was even passed off as the child of other parents. This still would not be a situation in which *this very woman* whom we call 'Elizabeth II' was the child of Mr. and Mrs. Truman, or so it seems to me. It would be a situation in which there was some other woman who had many of the properties that are in fact true of Elizabeth. Now, one question is, in this possible world, was Elizabeth herself ever born? Let's suppose she wasn't ever born. It would than be a situation in which, though Truman and his wife have a child with many of the properties of Elizabeth, Elizabeth herself didn't exist at all. One can only become convinced of this by reflection on how you would describe this situation. (That, I suppose, means in many cases that you won't become convinced of this, at least not at the moment. But it is something of which I personally have been convinced.)

How could a person originating from different parents, from a totally different sperm and egg, be *this very woman*? One can imagine, *given* the woman, that various things in her life could have changed: that she should have become a pauper; that her royal blood should have been unknown, and so on. One is given, let's say, a previous history of the world up to a certain time, and from that time it diverges considerably from the actual course. This seems to be possible. And so it's possible that even though she were born of these parents she never became queen. Even though she were born of these parents, like Mark Twain's character[54] she was switched off with another girl. But what is harder to imagine is her being born of different parents. It seems to me that anything coming from a different origin would not be this object.

In the case of this table,[55] we may not know what block of wood the table came from. Now could *this table* have been made from a completely *different* block of wood, or even of water cleverly hardened into ice—water taken from the Thames River? We could conceivably discover that, contrary to what we now think, this table is indeed made of ice from

[54] In *The Prince and The Pauper*.

[55] Of course I was pointing to a wooden table in the room.

the river. But let us suppose that it is not. Then, though we can imagine making a table out of another block of wood or even from ice, identical in appearance with this one, and though we could have put it in this very position in the room, it seems to me that this is *not* to imagine *this* table as made of wood or ice, but rather it is to imagine another table, *resembling* this one in all external details, made of another block of wood, or even of ice.[56, 57]

[56] A principle suggested by these examples is: *If a material object has its origin from a certain hunk of matter, it could not have had its origin in any other matter.* Some qualifications might have to be stated (for example, the vagueness of the notion of hunk of matter leads to some problems), but in a large class of cases the principle is perhaps susceptible of something like proof, using the principle of the necessity of identity for particulars. Let '$B$' be a name (rigid designator) of a table, let '$A$' name the piece of wood from which it actually came. Let '$C$' name another piece of wood. Then suppose $B$ were made from $A$, as in the actual world, but also another table $D$ were simultaneously made from $C$. (We assume that there is no relation between $A$ and $C$ which makes the possibility of making a table from one dependent on the possibility of making a table from the other.) Now in this situation $B \neq D$; hence, even if $D$ were made by itself, and no table were made from $A$, $D$ would not be $B$. Strictly speaking, the 'proof' uses the necessity of distinctness, not of identity. However, the same types of considerations that can be used to establish the latter can be used to establish the former. (Suppose $X \neq Y$; if $X$ and $Y$ were both identical to some object $Z$ in another possible world, then $X = Z$, $Y = Z$, hence $X = Y$.) Alternatively, the principle follows from the necessity of identity plus the 'Brouwersche' axiom, or, equivalently, symmetry of the accessibility relation between possible worlds. In any event, the argument applies only if the making of $D$ from $C$ does not affect the possibility of making $B$ from $A$, and vice-versa.

[57] In addition to the principle that the *origin* of an object is essential to it, another principle suggested is that the *substance* of which it is made is essential. Several complications exist here. First, one should not confuse the type of essence involved in the question 'What properties must an object retain if it is not to cease to exist, and what properties of the object can change while the object endures?', which is a temporal question, with the question 'What (timeless) properties could the object not have failed to have, and what properties could it have lacked while still (timelessly) existing?', which concerns necessity and not time and which is our topic here. Thus the question of whether the table could have *changed* into ice is irrelevant here. The question

These are only examples of essential properties.[58] I won't

---

whether the table could *originally* have been made of anything other than wood is relevant. Obviously this question is related to the necessity of the origin of the table from a given block of wood and whether that block, too, is essentially wood (even wood of a particular kind). Thus it is ordinarily impossible to imagine the table made from any substance other than the one of which it is actually made without going back through the entire history of the universe, a mind-boggling feat. (Other possibilities of the table not having been wooden originally have been suggested to me, including an ingenious suggestion of Slote's, but I find none of them really convincing. I cannot discuss them here.) A full discussion of the problems of essential properties of particulars is impossible here, but I will mention a few other points: (1) Ordinarily when we ask intuitively whether something might have happened to a given object, we ask whether the universe could have gone on as it actually did up to a certain time, but diverge in its history from that point forward so that the vicissitudes of that object would have been different from that time forth. *Perhaps* this feature should be erected into a general principle about essence. Note that the time in which the divergence from actual history occurs may be sometime before the object itself is actually created. For example, I might have been deformed if the fertilized egg from which I originated had been damaged in certain ways, even though I presumably did not yet exist at that time. (2) I am not suggesting that only origin and substantial makeup are essential. For example, if the very block of wood from which the table was made had instead been made into a vase, the table never would have existed. So (roughly) *being a table* seems to be an essential property of the table. (3) Just as the question whether an object *actually* has a certain property (e.g. baldness) can be vague, so the question whether the object essentially has a certain property can be vague, even when the question whether it actually has the property is decided. (4) Certain counterexamples to the origin principle appear to exist in ordinary parlance. I am convinced that they are not genuine counterexamples, but their exact analysis is difficult. I cannot discuss this here.

[58] Peter Geach has advocated (in *Mental Acts*, Routledge and Kegan Paul, London, 1957, Section 16, and elsewhere) a notion of 'nominal essence' different from the type of essential property considered here. According to Geach, since any act of pointing is ambiguous, someone who baptizes an object by pointing to it must apply a sortal property to disambiguate his reference and to ensure correct criteria of identity over time—for example, someone who assigns a reference to 'Nixon' by pointing to him must say, 'I use "Nixon" as a name of that *man*', thus removing his hearer's temptations to take him to be pointing to a nose or a time-slice. The sortal is then in some sense part of the meaning of the name; names do have a (partial) sense after all, though their senses may not be complete enough to determine their references,

dwell on them further because I want to go on to the more general case, which I mentioned in the last lecture, of some identities between terms for substances, and also the properties of substances and of natural kinds. Philosophers have, as I've said, been very interested in statements expressing theoretical identifications; among them, that light is a stream of photons, that water is $H_2O$, that lightning is an electrical discharge, that gold is the element with the atomic number 79.

To get clear about the status of these statements we must first maybe have some thoughts about the status of such substances as gold. What's gold? I don't know if this is an example which has particularly interested philosophers. Its interest in financial circles is diminishing because of increased stability of currencies.[59] Even so gold has interested many people. Here

---

as they are in description and cluster-of-descriptions theories. If I understand Geach correctly, his nominal essence should be understood in terms of a prioricity, not necessity, and thus is quite different from the kind of essence advocated here (perhaps this is part of what he means when he says he is dealing with 'nominal', not 'real', essences). So 'Nixon is a man', 'Dobbin is a horse', and the like would be *a priori* truths.

I need not take a position on this view here. But I would briefly mention the following: (1) Even if a sortal is used to disambiguate an ostensive reference, surely it need not be held *a priori* to be true of the object designated. Couldn't Dobbin turn out to belong to a species other than horses (though superficially he looked like a horse), Hesperus to be a planet rather than a star, or Lot's guests, even if he names them, to be angels rather than men? Perhaps Geach should stick to more cautious sortals. (2) Waiving the objection in (1), surely there is a substantial gap between premise and conclusion. Few speakers do in fact learn the reference of a given name by ostension; and, even if they picked up the name by a chain of communication leading back to an ostension, why should the sortal allegedly used in the ostension be, in any sense, part of the 'sense' of the name for them? No argument is offered here. (An extreme case: A mathematician's wife overhears her husband muttering the name 'Nancy'. She wonders whether Nancy, the thing to which her husband referred, is a woman or a Lie group. Why isn't her use of 'Nancy' a case of naming? If it isn't, the reason is *not* indefiniteness of her reference.)

[59] I may have spoken too soon. That is what some financial pages said when these lectures were delivered, January, 1970.

is what Immanuel Kant says about gold. (He was a wealthy speculator who kept his possessions under his bed.) Kant is introducing the distinction between analytic and synthetic judgements, and he says: 'All analytic judgements depend wholly on the law of contradiction, and are in their nature *a priori* cognitions, whether the concepts that supply them with matter be empirical or not. For the predicate of an affirmative analytic judgement is already contained in the concept of the subject, of which it cannot be denied without contradiction. . . . For this very reason all analytic judgements are *a priori* even when the concepts are empirical, as, for example, "Gold is a yellow metal"; for to know this I require no experience beyond my concept of gold as a yellow metal. It is, in fact, the very concept, and I need only analyze it without looking beyond it.'[60] I should have looked at the German. 'It is in fact the very concept' sounds as if Kant is saying here that 'gold' just *means* 'yellow metal'. If he says that, then it's especially strange, so let's suppose that that is not what he's saying. At least Kant thinks it's a *part* of the concept that gold is to be a yellow metal. He thinks we know this *a priori*, and that we could not possibly discover this to be empirically false.

Is Kant right about this? First, what I would have wanted to do would have been to discuss the part about gold being a metal. This, however, is complicated because first, I don't know too much chemistry. Investigating this a few days ago in just a couple of references, I found in a more phenomenological account of metals the statement that it's very difficult to say what a metal is. (It talks about malleability, ductility, and the like, but none of these exactly work.) On the other hand, something about the periodic table gave a description of

[60] *Prolegomena to Any Future Metaphysics*, Preamble Section 2.b. (Prussian Academy edition, p. 267). My impression of the passage was not changed by a subsequent cursory look at the German, though I can hardly lay claim to any real competence here.

elements as metals in terms of their valency properties. This may make some people think right away that there are really two concepts of metal operating here, a phenomenological one and a scientific one which then replaces it. This I reject, but since the move will tempt many, and can be refuted only after I develop my own views, it will not be suitable to use 'Gold is a metal' as an example to introduce these views.

But let's consider something easier—the question of the yellowness of gold. Could we discover that gold was not in fact yellow? Suppose an optical illusion were prevalent, due to peculiar properties of the atmosphere in South Africa and Russia and certain other areas where gold mines are common. Suppose there were an optical illusion which made the substance appear to be yellow; but, in fact, once the peculiar properties of the atmosphere were removed, we would see that it is actually blue. Maybe a demon even corrupted the vision of all those entering the gold mines (obviously their *souls* were already corrupt), and thus made them believe that this substance was yellow, though it is not. Would there on this basis be an announcement in the newspapers: 'It has turned out that there is no gold. Gold does not exist. What we took to be gold is not in fact gold.'? Just imagine the world financial crisis under these conditions! Here we have an undreamt of source of shakiness in the monetary system.

It seems to me that there would be no such announcement. On the contrary, what would be announced would be that though it appeared that gold was yellow, in fact gold has turned out not to be yellow, but blue. The reason is, I think, that we use 'gold' as a term for a certain *kind* of thing. Others have discovered this kind of thing and we have heard of it. We thus as part of a community of speakers have a certain connection between ourselves and a certain kind of thing. The kind of thing is *thought* to have certain identifying marks. Some of these marks may not really be true of gold. We might discover that we are wrong about them. Further, there might be a substance which has all the identifying marks we commonly attributed to gold and used to identify it in the first place, but which is not the same kind of thing, which is not the same substance. We would say of such a thing that though it has all the appearances we initially used to identify gold, it is not gold. Such a thing is, for example, as we well know, iron pyrites or fool's gold. This is not another kind of gold. It's a completely different thing which to the uninitiated person looks just like the substance which we discovered and called gold. We can say this not because we have changed the *meaning* of the term gold, and thrown in some other criteria which distinguished gold from pyrites. It seems to me that that's not true. On the contrary, we *discovered* that certain properties were true of gold in addition to the initial identifying marks by which we identified it. These properties, then, being characteristic of gold and not true of iron pyrites, show that the fool's gold is not in fact gold.

We should look at this in another example. It says somewhere in here:[61] 'I say "The word 'tiger' has meaning in English". . . . If I am then asked "What is a tiger?" I might reply "A tiger is a large carnivorous quadrupedal feline, tawny yellow in color with blackish transverse stripes and white belly," (derived from the entry under "tiger" in the *Shorter Oxford English Dictionary*.)' And now suppose someone says 'You have just said what the word "tiger" means in English.' And Ziff asks, 'Is that so?' and he says, correctly, 'I think not.' His example is, 'Suppose in a jungle clearing one says "look, a three-legged tiger!": must one be confused? The phrase "a three-legged tiger" is not a *contradictio in adjecto*. But if "tiger" in English meant, among other things, either quadruped or quadrupedal, the phrase "a three-legged tiger" could only be a

[61] Paul Ziff, *Semantic Analysis*, Ithaca, Cornell University Press, 1960, pp. 184–85.

*contradictio in adjecto.*' So, his example shows that if it is part of the concept of tiger that a tiger has four legs, there couldn't be a three-legged tiger. This is the sort of case which many philosophers tend to explain as a 'cluster concept'. Is it even a contradiction to suppose that we should discover that tigers *never* have four legs? Suppose the explorers who attributed these properties to tigers were deceived by an optical illusion, and that the animals they saw were from a three-legged species, would we then say that there turned out to be no tigers after all? I think we would say that in spite of the optical illusion which had deceived the explorers, tigers in fact have three legs.

Further, is it true that anything satisfying this description in the dictionary is necessarily a tiger? It seems to me that it is not. Suppose we discover an animal which, though having all external appearances of a tiger as described here, has an internal structure completely different from that of the tiger. Actually the word 'feline' was put in here, so it is not entirely fair. Let's suppose it were left out, for this example. That a tiger belongs to any particular biological family, anyway, was something we discovered. If 'feline' means just having the appearance of a cat, let's suppose that it does have the appearance of a big cat. We might find animals in some part of the world which, though they look just like a tiger, on examination were discovered not even to be mammals. Let's say they were in fact very peculiar looking reptiles. Do we then conclude on the basis of this description that some tigers are reptiles? We don't. We would rather conclude that these animals, though they have the external marks by which we originally identified tigers, are not in fact tigers, because they are not of the same species as the species which we called 'the species of tigers'. Now this, I think, is not because, as some people would say, the old concept of tiger has been replaced by a new scientific definition. I think this is true of the concept of tiger *before* the internal structure of tigers has been investigated. Even though we don't *know* the internal structure of tigers, we suppose—and let us suppose that we are right—that tigers form a certain species or natural kind. We then can imagine that there should be a creature which, though having all the external appearance of tigers, differs from them internally enough that we should say that it is not the same kind of thing. We can imagine it without knowing anything about this internal structure—what this internal structure is. We can say in advance that we use the term 'tiger' to designate a species, and that anything not of this species, even though it looks like a tiger, is not in fact a tiger.

Just as something may have all the properties by which we originally identified tigers and yet not be a tiger, so we might also find out tigers had *none* of the properties by which we originally identified them. Perhaps *none* are quadrupedal, none tawny yellow, none carnivorous, and so on; all these properties turn out to be based on optical illusions or other errors, as in the case of gold. So the term 'tiger', like the term 'gold', does *not* mark out a 'cluster concept' in which most, but perhaps not all, of the properties used to identify the kind must be satisfied. On the contrary, possession of most of these properties need not be a necessary condition for membership in the kind, nor need it be a sufficient condition.

Since we have found out that tigers do indeed, as we suspected, form a single kind, then something not of this kind is not a tiger. Of course, we may be mistaken in supposing that there is such a kind. In advance, we suppose that they probably do form a kind. Past experience has shown that usually things like this, living together, looking alike, mating together, do form a kind. If there are two kinds of tigers that have something to do with each other but not as much as we thought, then maybe they form a larger biological family. If they have absolutely nothing to do with each other, then there are really two kinds of tigers. This all depends on the history and on what we actually find out.

The philosopher I find most to recognize this sort of consideration (our thoughts on these matters developed independently) is Putnam. In an article called 'It Ain't Necessarily So',[62] he says of statements about species, that they are 'less necessary' (as he cautiously says) than statements like 'bachelors aren't married'. The example he gives is 'cats are animals'. Cats might turn out to be automata, or strange demons (not his example) planted by a magician. Suppose they turned out to be a species of demons. Then on his view, and I think also my view, the inclination is to say, not that there turned out to be no cats, but that cats have turned out not to be animals as we originally supposed. The original concept of cat is: *that kind of thing*, where the kind can be identified by paradigmatic instances. It is not something picked out by any qualitative dictionary definition. However, Putnam's conclusion is that statements like 'cats are animals' are 'less necessary' than statements like 'bachelors are unmarried'. Certainly I agree that the argument indicates that such statements are not known *a priori*, and hence are not analytic;[63] whether a given kind is a

[62] *Journal of Philosophy*, 59, No. 22 (October 25, 1962), pp. 658–71. In subsequent work on natural kinds and physical properties, which I have not had a chance to see at the time of this writing, Putnam has done further work, which (I gather) has many points of contact with the viewpoint expressed here. As I mentioned in the text, there are some divergencies between Putnam's approach and mine; Putnam does not base his considerations on the apparatus of necessary versus *a priori* truths which I invoke. In his earlier paper, 'The Analytic and the Synthetic', *Minnesota Studies in the Philosophy of Science*, vol. III, pp. 358–97, he seems closer to the 'cluster concept' theory in some respects, suggesting, for example, that it applies to proper names.

I should emphasize again that it was an example of Rogers Albritton which called my attention to this complex of problems, though Albritton probably would not accept the theories I have developed on the basis of the example.

[63] I am presupposing that an analytic truth is one which depends on *meanings* in the strict sense and therefore is necessary as well as *a priori*. If statements whose *a priori* truth is known via the fixing of a reference are counted as analytic, then some analytic truths are contingent; this possibility is excluded in the notion of analyticity adopted here. The ambiguity in the notion of

species of animals is a matter for empirical investigation. Perhaps this epistemological sense is what Putnam means by 'necessary'. The question remains whether such statements are necessary in the non-epistemological sense advocated in these lectures. So the next thing to investigate is (using the concept of necessity that I talked about): are such statements as 'cats are animals', or such statements as 'gold is a yellow metal', necessary?

So far I've only been talking about what we could find out. I've been saying we could find out that gold was not in fact yellow, contrary to what we thought. If one went in more detail into the concept of metals, let's say in terms of valency properties, one could certainly find out that though one took gold to be a metal, gold is not in fact a metal. Is it necessary or contingent that gold be a metal? I don't want to go into detail on the concept of a metal—as I said, I don't know enough about it. Gold apparently has the atomic number 79. Is it a necessary or a contingent property of gold that it has the atomic number 79? Certainly we could find out that we were mistaken. The whole theory of protons, of atomic numbers, the whole theory of molecular structure and of atomic structure, on which such views are based, could *all* turn out to be false. Certainly we didn't know it from time immemorial. So in that sense, gold could turn out not to have atomic number 79.

Given that gold *does* have the atomic number 79, could something be gold without having the atomic number 79?

---

analyticity of course arises from the ambiguity in the usual uses of such terms as 'definition' and 'sense'. I have not attempted to deal with the delicate problems regarding analyticity in these lectures, but I will say that some (though not all) of the cases often adduced to discredit the analytic-synthetic distinction, especially those involving natural phenomena and natural kinds, should be handled in terms of the apparatus of fixing a reference invoked here. Note that Kant's example, 'gold is a yellow metal', is not even *a priori*, and whatever necessity it has is established by scientific investigation; it is thus far from analytic in any sense.

Let us suppose the scientists have investigated the nature of gold and have found that it is part of the very nature of this substance, so to speak, that it have the atomic number 79. Suppose we now find some other yellow metal, or some other yellow thing, with all the properties by which we originally identified gold, and many of the additional ones that we have discovered later. An example of one with many of the initial properties is iron pyrites, 'fool's gold.' As I have said, we wouldn't say that this substance is gold. So far we are speaking of the actual world. Now consider a possible world. Consider a counterfactual situation in which, let us say, fool's gold or iron pyrites was actually found in various mountains in the United States, or in areas of South Africa and the Soviet Union. Suppose that all the areas which actually contain gold now, contained pyrites instead, or some other substance which counterfeited the superficial properties of gold but lacked its atomic structure.[64] Would we say, of this counterfactual situation, that in that situation gold would not even have been an element (because pyrites is not an element)? It seems to me that we would not. We would instead describe this as a situation in which a substance, say iron pyrites, which is not gold, would have been found in the very mountains which actually contain gold and would have had the very properties by which we commonly identify gold. But it would not be gold; it would be something else. One should *not* say that it would still be gold in this possible world, though gold would then lack the atomic number 79. It would be some other stuff, some other substance. (Once again, whether people counterfactually would have *called* it 'gold' is irrelevant. *We* do not describe it as gold.) And so, it seems to me, this would not be a case in which possibly gold might not have been an

[64] Even better pairs of ringers exist; for example, some pairs of elements of a single column in the periodic table which resemble each other closely but nevertheless are different elements.

element, nor can there be such a case (except in the epistemic sense of 'possible'). Given that gold *is* this element, any other substance, even though it looks like gold and is found in the very places where we in fact find gold, would not be gold. It would be some other substance which was a counterfeit for gold. In any counterfactual situation where the same geographical areas were filled with such a substance, they would not have been filled with gold. They would have been filled with something else.

So if this consideration is right, it tends to show that such statements representing scientific discoveries about what this stuff *is* are not contingent truths but necessary truths in the strictest possible sense. It's not just that it's a scientific law, but of course we can imagine a world in which it would fail. Any world in which we imagine a substance which does not have these properties is a world in which we imagine a substance which is not gold, provided these properties form the basis of what the substance is. In particular, then, present scientific theory is such that it is part of the nature of gold as we have it to be an element with atomic number 79. It will therefore be necessary and not contingent that gold be an element with atomic number 79. (We may also in the same way, then, investigate further how color and metallic properties follow from what we have found the substance gold to be: to the extent that such properties follow from the atomic structure of gold, they are necessary properties of it, even though they unquestionably are not part of the *meaning* of 'gold' and were not known with *a priori* certainty.)

Putnam's example 'cats are animals' comes under the same sort of heading. We have in fact made a very surprising discovery in this case. We have in fact found nothing to go against our belief. Cats are in fact animals! Then is this truth a necessary truth or a contingent one? It seems to me that it is necessary. Consider the counterfactual situation in which in place of these creatures—these animals—we have in fact little demons which when they approached us brought bad luck indeed. Should we describe this as a situation in which cats were demons? It seems to me that these demons would not be cats. They would be demons in a cat-like form. We could have discovered that the actual cats that we *have* are demons. Once we have discovered, however, that they are *not*, it is part of their very nature that, when we describe a counterfactual world in which there were such demons around, we must say that the demons would not be cats. It would be a world containing demons masquerading as cats. Although we could say cats *might turn out* to be demons, of a certain species, given that cats are in fact animals, any cat-like being which is not an animal, in the actual world or in a counterfactual one, is not a cat. The same holds even for animals with the appearance of cats but reptilic internal structure. Were such to exist, they would not be cats, but 'fool's cats'.

This has some relation also to the essence of a particular object. The molecular theory has discovered, let's say, that this object here is composed of molecules. This was certainly an important empirical discovery. It was something we didn't know in advance; maybe this might have been composed, for all we knew, of some ethereal entelechy. Now imagine an object occupying this very position in the room which *was* an ethereal entelechy. Would it be this very object here? It might have all the appearance of this object, but it seems to me that it could not ever be *this thing*. The vicissitudes of *this thing* might have been very different from its actual history. It might have been transported to the Kremlin. It might have already been hewn into bits and no longer exist at the present time. Various things might have happened to it. But whatever we imagine counterfactually having happened to it other than what actually did, the one thing we cannot imagine happening to this thing is that *it*, given that it is composed of molecules, should still have existed and not have been composed of molecules. We can imagine having discovered that it wasn't composed of molecules. But once we know that this is a thing composed of molecules—that this is the very nature of the substance of which it is made—we can't then, at least if the way I see it is correct, imagine that this thing might have failed to have been composed of molecules.

According to the view I advocate, then, terms for natural kinds are much closer to proper names than is ordinarily supposed. The old term 'common name' is thus quite appropriate for predicates marking out species or natural kinds, such as 'cow' or 'tiger'. My considerations apply also, however, to certain mass terms for natural kinds, such as 'gold', 'water', and the like. It is interesting to compare my views to those of Mill. Mill counts both predicates like 'cow', definite descriptions, and proper names as names. He says of 'singular' names that they are connotative if they are definite descriptions but non-connotative if they are proper names. On the other hand, Mill says that *all* 'general' names are connotative; such a predicate as 'human being' is defined as the conjunction of certain properties which give necessary and sufficient conditions for humanity—rationality, animality, and certain physical features.[65] The modern logical tradition, as represented by Frege and Russell, seems to hold that Mill was wrong about singular names, but right about general names. More recent philosophy has followed suit, except that, in the case of both proper names and natural kind terms, it often replaces the notion of defining properties by that of a cluster of properties, only some of which need to be satisfied in each particular case. My own view, on the other hand, regards Mill as more-or-less right about 'singular' names, but wrong about 'general' names. *Perhaps* some 'general' names ('foolish', 'fat', 'yellow') express

[65] Mill, op. cit.

properties.[66] In a significant sense, such general names as 'cow' and 'tiger' do not, unless *being a cow* counts trivially as a property. Certainly 'cow' and 'tiger' are *not* short for the conjunction of properties a dictionary would take to define them, as Mill thought. Whether science can discover empirically that certain properties are *necessary* of cows, or of tigers, is another question, which I answer affirmatively.

Let's consider how this applies to the types of identity statements expressing scientific discoveries that I talked about before—say, that water is $H_2O$. It certainly represents a discovery that water is $H_2O$. We identified water originally by its characteristic feel, appearance and perhaps taste, (though the taste may usually be due to the impurities). If there were a substance, even actually, which had a completely different atomic structure from that of water, but resembled water in these respects, would we say that some water wasn't $H_2O$? I think not. We would say instead that just as there is a fool's gold there could be a fool's water; a substance which, though having the properties by which we originally identified water, would not in fact be water. And this, I think, applies not only to the actual world but even when we talk about counterfactual situations. If there had been a substance, which was a fool's water, it would then be fool's water and not water. On the other hand if this substance can take another form—such

[66] I am not going to give any criterion for what I mean by a 'pure property', or Fregean intension. It is hard to find unquestionable examples of what is meant. Yellowness certainly expresses a manifest physical property of an object and, relative to the discussion of gold above, can be regarded as a property in the required sense. Actually, however, it is not without a certain referential element of its own, for on the present view yellowness is picked out and rigidly designated as that external physical property of the object which we sense by means of the *visual impression of yellowness*. It does in this respect resemble the natural kind terms. The phenomenological quality of the sensation itself, on the other hand, can be regarded as a *quale* in some pure sense. Perhaps I am rather vague about these questions, but further precision seems unnecessary here.

as the polywater allegedly discovered in the Soviet Union, with very different identifying marks from that of what we now call water—it is a form of water because it is the same substance, even though it doesn't have the appearances by which we originally identified water.

Let's consider the statement 'Light is a stream of photons' or 'Heat is the motion of molecules'. By referring to light, of course, I mean something which we have some of in this room. When I refer to heat, I refer not to an internal sensation that someone may have, but to an external phenomenon which we perceive through the sense of feeling; it produces a characteristic sensation which we call the sensation of heat. Heat *is* the motion of molecules. We have also discovered that increasing heat corresponds to increasing motion of molecules, or, strictly speaking, increasing average kinetic energy of molecules. So temperature is identified with mean molecular kinetic energy. However I won't talk about temperature because there is the question of how the actual scale is to be set. It might just be set in terms of the mean molecular kinetic energy.[67] But what represents an interesting phenomenological discovery is that when it's hotter the molecules are moving faster. We have also discovered about light that light is a stream of photons; alternatively it is a form of electromagnetic radiation. Originally we identified light by the characteristic internal visual impressions it can produce in us, that make us able to see. Heat, on the other hand, we originally identified by the characteristic effect on one aspect of our nerve endings or our sense of touch.

Imagine a situation in which human beings were blind or their eyes didn't work. They were unaffected by light. Would that have been a situation in which light did not exist? It seems

[67] Of course, there is the question of the relation of the statistical mechanical notion of temperature to, for example, the thermodynamic notion. I wish to leave such questions aside in this discussion.

to me that it would not. It would have been a situation in which our eyes were not sensitive to light. Some creatures may have eyes not sensitive to light. Among such creatures are unfortunately some people, of course; they are called 'blind'. Even if all people had had awful vestigial growths and just couldn't see a thing, the light might have been around; but it would not have been able to affect people's eyes in the proper way. So it seems to me that such a situation would be a situation in which there was light, but people could not see it. So, though we may identify light by the characteristic visual impressions it produces in us, this seems to be a good example of fixing a reference. We fix what light is by the fact that it is whatever, out in the world, affects our eyes in a certain way. But now, talking about counterfactual situations in which let's say, people were blind, we would not then say that since, in such situations, nothing could affect their eyes, light would not exist; rather we would say that that would be a situation in which light—the thing we have identified as that which in fact enables us to see—existed but did not manage to help us see due to some defect in us.

Perhaps we can imagine that, by some miracle, sound waves somehow enabled some creature to see. I mean, they gave him visual impressions just as we have, maybe exactly the same color sense. We can also imagine the same creature to be completely *insensitive* to light (photons). Who knows what subtle undreamt of possibilities there may be? Would we say that in such a possible world, it was sound which was light, that these wave motions in the air were light? It seems to me that, given our concept of light, we should describe the situation differently. It would be a situation in which certain creatures, maybe even those who were called 'people' and inhabited this planet, were sensitive not to light but to sound waves, sensitive to them in exactly the same way that we are sensitive to light. If this is so, once we have found out what light is, when we talk about other possible worlds we are talking about *this* phenomenon in the world, and not using 'light' as a phrase *synonymous* with 'whatever gives us the visual impression—whatever helps us to see'; for there might have been light and it not helped us to see; and even something else might have helped us to see. The way we identified light *fixed a reference.*

And similarly for other such phrases, such as 'heat'. Here heat is something which we have identified (and fixed the reference of its name) by its giving a certain sensation, which we call 'the sensation of heat'. We don't have a special name for this sensation other than as a sensation of heat. It's interesting that the language is this way. Whereas you might suppose it, from what I am saying, to have been the other way. At any rate, we identify heat and are able to sense it by the fact that it produces in us a sensation of heat. It might here be so important to the concept that its reference is fixed in this way, that if someone else detects heat by some sort of instrument, but is unable to feel it, we might want to say, if we like, that the concept of heat is not the same even though the referent is the same.

Nevertheless, the term 'heat' doesn't *mean* 'whatever gives people these sensations'. For first, people might not have been sensitive to heat, and yet the heat still have existed in the external world. Secondly, let us suppose that somehow light rays, because of some difference in their nerve endings, *did* give them these sensations. It would not then be heat but light which gave people the sensation which we call the sensation of heat.

Can we then imagine a possible world in which heat was not molecular motion? We can imagine, of course, having discovered that it was not. It seems to me that any case which someone will think of, which he thinks at first is a case in which heat—contrary to what is actually the case—would have been something other than molecular motion, would actually be a case in which some creatures with different nerve endings from ours inhabit this planet (maybe even we, if it's a contingent fact about us that we have this particular neural structure), and in which these creatures were sensitive to that something else, say light, in such a way that they felt the same thing that we feel when we feel heat. But this is not a situation in which, say, light would have been heat, or even in which a stream of photons would have been heat, but a situation in which a stream of photons would have produced the characteristic sensations which *we* call 'sensations of heat'.

Similarly for many other such identifications, say, that lightning is electricity. Flashes of lightning are flashes of electricity. Lightning is an electrical discharge. We can imagine, of course, I suppose, other ways in which the sky might be illuminated at night with the same sort of flash without any electrical discharge being present. Here too, I am inclined to say, when we imagine this, we imagine something with all the visual appearances of lightning but which is not, in fact, lightning. One could be told: this appeared to be lightning but it was not. I suppose this might even happen now. Someone might, by a clever sort of apparatus, produce some phenomenon in the sky which would fool people into thinking that there was lightning even though in fact no lightning was present. And you wouldn't say that that phenomenon, because it looks like lightning, was in fact lightning. It was a different phenomenon from lightning, which is the phenomenon of an electrical discharge; and this is not lightning but just something that deceives us into thinking that there is lightning.

What characteristically goes on in these cases of, let's say, 'heat is molecular motion'? There is a certain referent which we have fixed, for the real world and for all possible worlds, by a contingent property of it, namely the property that it's able to produce such and such sensations in us. Let's say it's a contingent property of heat that it produces such and such sensations in people. It's after all contingent that there should ever have been people on this planet at all. So one doesn't know *a priori* what physical phenomenon, described in other terms—in basic terms of physical theory—is the phenomenon which produces these sensations. We don't know this, and we've discovered eventually that this phenomenon is in fact molecular motion. When we have discovered this, we've discovered an identification which gives us an essential property of this phenomenon. We have discovered a phenomenon which in all possible worlds will be molecular motion—which could not have failed to be molecular motion, because that's what the phenomenon *is*.[68] On the other hand, the property by which we identify it originally, that of producing such and such a sensation in us, is not a necessary property but a contingent one. This very phenomenon could have existed, but due to differences in our neural structures and so on, have failed to be felt as heat. Actually, when I say *our* neural structures, as those of human beings, I'm really hedging a point which I made earlier; because of course, it might be part of the very nature of human beings that they have a neural structure which is sensitive to heat. Therefore this too could turn out to be necessary if enough investigation showed it. This I'm just ignoring, for the purpose of simplifying the discussion. At any rate it's not necessary, I suppose, that this

[68] Some people have been inclined to argue that although certainly we cannot say that sound waves 'would have been heat' if they had been felt by the sensation which we feel when we feel heat, the situation is different with respect to a possible phenomenon, not present in the actual world, and distinct from molecular motion. Perhaps, it is suggested, there might be another form of heat other than 'our heat', which was not molecular motion; though no actual phenomenon other than molecular motion, such as sound, would qualify. Similar claims have been made for gold and for light. Although I am disinclined to accept these views, they would make relatively little difference to the substance of the present lectures. Someone who is inclined to hold these views can simply replace the terms 'light', 'heat', 'pain', etc., in the examples by 'our light', 'our heat', 'our pain' and the like. I therefore will not take the space to discuss this issue here.

planet should have been inhabited by creatures sensitive to heat in this way.

I will conclude with some remarks about the application of the foregoing considerations to the debate over the mind-body identity thesis. Before I do so, however, I wish to recapitulate the views I have developed, and perhaps add a point or two.

First, my argument implicitly concludes that certain general terms, those for natural kinds, have a greater kinship with proper names than is generally realized. This conclusion holds for certain for various species names, whether they are count nouns, such as 'cat', 'tiger', 'chunk of gold', or mass terms such as 'gold', 'water', 'iron pyrites'. It also applies to certain terms for natural phenomena, such as 'heat', 'light', 'sound', 'lightning', and, presumably, suitably elaborated, to corresponding adjectives—'hot', 'loud', 'red'.

Mill, as I have recalled, held that although some 'singular names', the definite descriptions, have both denotation and connotation, others, the genuine proper names, had denotation but not connotation. Mill further maintained that 'general names', or general terms, had connotation. Such terms as 'cow' or 'human' are defined by the conjunction of certain properties which pick out their extension—a human being, for example, is a rational animal with certain physical characteristics. The hoary tradition of definition by *genus* and *differentia* is of a piece with such a conception. If Kant did, indeed, suppose that 'gold' could be *defined* as 'yellow metal', it may well be this tradition which led him to the definition. ('Metal' would be the genus, 'yellow' the differentia. The differentia could hardly include 'being gold' without circularity.)

The modern logical tradition, as represented by Frege and Russell, disputed Mill on the issue of singular names, but endorsed him on that of general names. Thus *all* terms, both singular and general, have a 'connotation' or Fregean sense. More recent theorists have followed Frege and Russell, modifying their views only by replacing the notion of a sense as given by a particular conjunction of properties with that of a sense as given by a 'cluster' of properties, only *enough* of which need apply. The present view, directly reversing Frege and Russell, (more or less) *endorses* Mill's view of *singular* terms, but *disputes* his view of *general* terms.

Second, the present view asserts, in the case of species terms as in that of proper names, that one should bear in mind the contrast between the *a priori* but perhaps contingent properties carried with a term, given by the way its reference was fixed, and the analytic (and hence necessary) properties a term may carry, given by its meaning. For species, as for proper names, the way the reference of a term is fixed should not be regarded as a synonym for the term. In the case of proper names, the reference can be fixed in various ways. In an initial baptism it is typically fixed by an ostension or a description. Otherwise, the reference is usually determined by a chain, passing the name from link to link. The same observations hold for such a general term as 'gold'. If we imagine a hypothetical (admittedly somewhat artificial) baptism of the substance, we must imagine it picked out as by some such 'definition' as, 'Gold is the substance instantiated by the items over there, or at any rate, by almost all of them'. Several features of this baptism are worthy of note. First, the identity in the 'definition' does not express a (completely) necessary truth: though each of these items is, indeed, essentially (necessarily) gold,[69] gold might have existed even if the items did not. The definition does, however, express an *a priori* truth, in the same sense as (and with the same qualifications applied as) '1 meter = length of $S$': it *fixes a reference*. I believe that, in general,

[69] Assuming, of course, that they are all gold; as I say below, some may be fool's gold. We know in advance, *a priori*, that it is not the case that the items are *typically* fool's gold; and all those items which are actually gold are, of course, essentially gold.

terms for natural kinds (e.g., animal, vegetable, and chemical kinds) get their reference fixed in this way; the substance is defined as the kind instantiated by (almost all of) a given sample. The 'almost all' qualification allows that some fools' gold may be present in the sample. If the original sample has a small number of deviant items, they will be rejected as not really gold. If, on the other hand, the supposition that there is one uniform substance or kind in the initial sample proves more radically in error, reactions can vary: sometimes we may declare that there are two kinds of gold, sometimes we may drop the term 'gold'. (These possibilities are not supposed to be exhaustive.) And the alleged new kind may prove illusory for other reasons. For example, suppose some items (let the set of them be *I*) are discovered and are believed to belong to a new kind *K*. Suppose that later it is discovered that the items in *I* are indeed of a single kind; however, they belong to a previously known kind, *L*. Observational error led to the false initial belief that the items in *I* possessed some characteristic *C* excluding them from *L*. In this case we would surely say that the kind *K* does not exist, in spite of the fact that it was defined by reference to a uniform initial sample. (Note that if *L* had not previously been identified, we might well have said that the kind *K* did exist, but that we were in error in supposing it to be associated with the characteristic *C*!) To the extent that the notion 'same kind' is vague, so is the original notion of gold. Ordinarily, the vagueness doesn't matter in practice.

In the case of a natural phenomenon perceptible to the senses, the way the reference is picked out is simple: 'Heat = that which is sensed by sensation *S*'. Once again, the identity fixes a reference: it therefore is *a priori*, but not necessary, since heat might have existed, though we did not. 'Heat', like 'gold', is a rigid designator, whose reference is fixed by its 'definition'. Other natural phenomena, such as electricity, are originally identified as the causes of certain concrete experimental effects. I do not attempt to give exhaustive characterizations here, only examples.

Third, in the case of natural kinds, certain properties, believed to be at least roughly characteristic of the kind and believed to apply to the original sample, are used to place new items, outside the original sample, in the kind. ('Properties' is used here in a broad sense, and may include larger kinds: for example animality and felinity, for tigers.) These properties need not hold *a priori* of the kind; later empirical investigation may establish that some of the properties did not belong to the original sample, or that they were peculiarities of the original sample, not to be generalized to the kind as a whole. (Thus the yellowness of gold may be an optical illusion; or, more plausibly, though the gold originally observed was indeed yellow, it could turn out that some gold is white.) On the other hand, an item may possess all the characteristics originally used and fail to belong to the kind. Thus an animal may look just like a tiger, and fail to be a tiger, as mentioned above; distinct elements in the same column of the periodic table may resemble each other rather closely. Such failures are the exception; but, as in the periodic table, they *do* arise. (Sometimes a failure of the initial sample to have the characteristics associated with it may lead us to repudiate the species, as in the *I-K-L* case above. But this phenomenon is not typical, let alone universal; see the remarks on the yellowness of gold, or whether cats are animals.) *A priori*, all we can say is that it is am empirical matter whether the characteristics originally associated with the kind apply to its members universally, or even ever, and whether they are in fact jointly sufficient for membership in the kind. (The joint sufficiency is extremely unlikely to be *necessary*, but it may be *true*. In fact, any animal looking just like a tiger is a tiger—as far as I know—though it is (metaphysically) *possible* that there should have been animals that resembled tigers but were not tigers. The universal applicability, on the other hand, may well be necessary, if true. 'Cats are animals' *has* turned out to be a necessary truth. Indeed of many such statements, especially those subsuming one species under another, we know *a priori* that, if they are true at all, they are necessarily true.)

Fourth, scientific investigation generally discovers characteristics of gold which are far better than the original set. For example, it turns out that a material object is (pure) gold if and only if the only element contained therein is that with atomic number 79. Here, the 'if and only if' can be taken to be *strict* (necessary). In general, science attempts, by investigating basic structural traits, to find the nature, and thus the essence (in the philosophical sense) of the kind. The case of natural phenomena is similar; such theoretical identifications as 'heat is molecular motion' are *necessary*, though not *a priori*. The type of property identity used in science seems to be associated with *necessity*, not with a prioricity, or analyticity: For all bodies $x$ and $y$, $x$ is hotter than $y$ if and only if $x$ has higher mean molecular kinetic energy than $y$. Here the coextensiveness of the predicates is *necessary*, but not *a priori*. The philosophical notion of attribute, on the other hand, seems to demand *a priori* (and analytic) coextensiveness as well as necessary coextensiveness.

Note that on the present view, scientific discoveries of species essence do not constitute a 'change of meaning'; the possibility of such discoveries was part of the original enterprise. We need not even assume that the biologist's denial that whales are fish shows his 'concept of fishhood' to be different from that of the layman; he simply corrects the layman, discovering that 'whales are mammals, not fish' is a necessary truth. Neither 'whales are mammals' *nor* 'whales are fish' was supposed to be *a priori* or analytic in any case.

Fifth, and independently of the scientific investigations just mentioned, the 'original sample' gets augmented by the discovery of new items.[70] (In the case of gold, men applied tremendous effort to the task. Those who doubt the natural scientific curiosity of Man should consider this case. Only such anti-scientific fundamentalists as Bryan cast aspersions on the effort.) More important, the species-name may be passed from link to link, exactly as in the case of proper names, so that many who have seen little or no gold can still use the term. Their reference is determined by a causal (historical) chain, not by use of any items. I will make even less effort here to spell out an exact theory than in the case of proper names.

Usually, when a proper name is passed from link to link, the way the reference of the name is fixed is of little importance to us. It matters not at all that different speakers may fix the reference of the name in different ways, provided that they give it the same referent. The situation is probably not very different for species names, though the temptation to think that the metallurgist has a different concept of gold from the man who has never seen any may be somewhat greater. The interesting fact is that the way the reference is fixed seems overwhelmingly important to us in the case of sensed phenomena: a blind man who uses the term 'light', even though he uses it as a rigid designator for the very same phenomenon as we, seems to us to have lost a great deal, perhaps enough for us to declare that he has a different concept. ('Concept' here is used non-technically!) The fact that we identify light in a certain way seems to us to be *crucial*, even though it is not necessary; the intimate connection may create an *illusion* of necessity. I think that this observation, together with the remarks on property-identity above, may well be essential to an under-

[70] Obviously, there are also artificialities in this whole account. For example, it may be hard to say which items constitute the original sample. Gold may have been discovered independently by various people at various times. I do not feel that any such complications will radically alter the picture.

standing of the traditional disputes over primary and secondary qualities.[71]

Let us return to the question of theoretical identification. Theoretical identities, according to the conception I advocate, are generally identities involving two rigid designators and therefore are examples of the necessary *a posteriori*. Now in spite of the arguments I gave before for the distinction between necessary and *a priori* truth, the notion of *a posteriori* necessary truth may still be somewhat puzzling. Someone may well be inclined to argue as follows: 'You have admitted that heat might have turned out not to have been molecular motion, and that gold might have turned out not to have been the element with the atomic number 79. For that matter, you also

[71] To understand this dispute, it is especially important to realize that yellowness is not a dispositional property, although it is related to a disposition. Many philosophers for want of any other theory of the meaning of the term 'yellow', have been inclined to regard it as expressing a dispositional property. At the same time, I suspect many have been bothered by the 'gut feeling' that yellowness is a manifest property, just as much 'right out there' as hardness or spherical shape. The proper account, on the present conception is, of course, that the reference of 'yellowness' is fixed by the description 'that (manifest) property of objects which causes them, under normal circumstances, to be seen as yellow (i.e., to be sensed by certain visual impressions)'; 'yellow', of course, does not *mean* 'tends to produce such and such a sensation'; if we had had different neutral structures, if atmospheric conditions had been different, if we had been blind, and so on, then yellow objects would have done no such thing. If one tries to revise the definition of 'yellow' to be, 'tends to produce such and such visual impressions under circumstances *C*', then one will find that the specification of the circumstances *C* either circularly involves yellowness or plainly makes the alleged definition into a scientific discovery rather than a synonymy. If we take the 'fixes a reference' view, then it is up to the physical scientist to identify the property so marked out in any more fundamental physical terms that he wishes.

Some philosophers have argued that such terms as 'sensation of yellow', 'sensation of heat', 'sensation of pain', and the like, could not be in the language unless they were identifiable in terms of external observable phenomena, such as heat, yellowness, and associated human behavior. I think that this question is independent of any view argued in the text.

have acknowledged that Elizabeth II might have turned out not to be the daughter of George VI, or even to originate in the particular sperm and egg we had thought, and this table might have turned out to be made from ice made from water from the Thames. I gather that Hesperus might have turned out not to be Phosphorus. What then can you mean when you say that such eventualities are impossible? If Hesperus might have *turned out* not to be Phosphorus, then Hesperus might not have *been* Phosphorus. And similarly for the other cases: if the world could have *turned out* otherwise, it could have *been* otherwise. To deny this fact is to deny the self-evident modal principle that what is entailed by a possibility must itself be possible. Nor can you evade the difficulty by declaring the "might have" of "might have turned out otherwise" to be merely epistemic, in the way that "Fermat's Last Theorem might turn out to be true and might turn out to be false" merely expresses our present ignorance, and "Arithmetic might have turned out to be complete" signals our former ignorance. In these mathematical cases, we may have been ignorant, but it was in fact mathematically impossible for the answer to turn out other than it did. Not so in your favorite cases of essence and of identity between two rigid designators: it really is logically possible that gold should have turned out to be a compound, and this table might really have turned out not to be made of wood, let alone of a given particular block of wood. The contrast with the mathematical case could not be greater and would not be alleviated even if, as you suggest, there may be mathematical truths which it is impossible to know *a priori*.'

Perhaps anyone who has caught the spirit of my previous remarks can give my answer himself, but there is a clarification of my previous discussion which is relevant here. The objector is correct when he argues that if I hold that this table could not have been made of ice, then I must also hold that it could not have turned out to be made of ice; *it could have turned out that P* entails that *P* could have been the case. What, then, does the intuition that the table might have turned out to have been made of ice or of anything else, that it might even have turned out not to be made of molecules, amount to? I think that it means simply that there might have been *a table* looking and feeling just like this one and placed in this very position in the room, which was in fact made of ice. In other words, I (or some conscious being) could have been *qualitatively in the same epistemic situation* that in fact obtains, I could have the same sensory evidence that I in fact have, about *a table* which was made of ice. The situation is thus akin to the one which inspired the counterpart theorists; when I speak of the possibility of the table turning out to be made of various things, I am speaking loosely. *This* table itself could not have had an origin different from the one it in fact had, but in a situation qualitatively identical to this one with respect to all the evidence I had in advance, the room could have contained *a table made of ice* in place of this one. Something like counterpart theory is thus applicable to the situation, but it applies only because we are *not* interested in what might have been true of *this particular* table, but in what might or might not be true of *a table* given certain evidence. It is precisely because it is *not* true that this table might have been made of ice from the Thames that we must turn here to qualitative descriptions and counterparts. To apply these notions to genuine *de re* modalities is, from the present standpoint, perverse.

The general answer to the objector can be stated, then, as follows: Any necessary truth, whether *a priori* or *a posteriori*, could not have turned out otherwise. In the case of some necessary *a posteriori* truths, however, we can say that under appropriate qualitatively identical evidential situations, an appropriate corresponding qualitative statement might have been false. The loose and inaccurate statement that gold might have turned out to be a compound should be replaced (roughly) by the statement that it is logically possible that there should have been a compound with all the properties originally known to hold of gold. The inaccurate statement that Hesperus might have turned out not to be Phosphorus should be replaced by the true contingency mentioned earlier in these lectures: two distinct bodies might have occupied, in the morning and the evening, respectively, the very positions actually occupied by Hesperus-Phosphorus-Venus.[72] The reason the example of Fermat's Last Theorem gives a different impression is that here no analogue suggests itself, except for the extremely general statement that, in the absence of proof or disproof, it is possible for *a mathematical conjecture* to be either true or false.

I have not given any general paradigm for the appropriate corresponding qualitative contingent statement. Since we are concerned with how things might have turned out otherwise, our general paradigm is to redescribe both the prior evidence and the statement qualitatively and claim that they are only contingently related. In the case of identities, using two rigid designators, such as the Hesperus-Phosphorus case above, there is a simpler paradigm which is often usable to at least approximately the same effect. Let '$R_1$' and '$R_2$' be the two rigid designators which flank the identity sign. Then '$R_1 = R_2$' is necessary if true. The references of '$R_1$' and '$R_2$', respectively, may well be fixed by nonrigid designators '$D_1$' and '$D_2$', in the Hesperus and Phosphorus cases these have the form 'the heavenly body in such-and-such position in the sky in the evening (morning)'. Then although '$R_1 = R_2$' is necessary,

[72] Some of the statements I myself make above may be loose and inaccurate in this sense. If I say, 'Gold *might* turn out not to be an element,' I speak correctly; 'might' here is *epistemic* and expresses the fact that the evidence does not justify *a priori* (Cartesian) certainty that gold is an element. I am also strictly correct when I say that the elementhood of gold was discovered *a posteriori*. If I say, 'Gold *might have* turned out not to be an element,' I seem to mean this metaphysically and my statement is subject to the correction noted in the text.

'$D_1 = D_2$' may well be contingent, and this is often what leads to the erroneous view that '$R_1 = R_2$' might have turned out otherwise.

I finally turn to an all too cursory discussion of the application of the foregoing considerations to the identity thesis. Identity theorists have been concerned with several distinct types of identifications: of a person with his body, of a particular sensation (or event or state of having the sensation) with a particular brain state (Jones's pain at 06 : 00 was his C-fiber stimulation at that time), and of *types* of mental states with the corresponding *types* of physical states (pain is the stimulation of C-fibers). Each of these, and other types of identifications in the literature, present analytical problems, rightly raised by Cartesian critics, which cannot be avoided by a simple appeal to an alleged confusion of synonymy with identity. I should mention that there is of course no obvious bar, at least (I say cautiously) none which should occur to any intelligent thinker on a first reflection just before bedtime, to advocacy of some identity theses while doubting or denying others. For example, some philosophers have accepted the identity of particular sensations with particular brain states while denying the possibility of identities between mental and physical *types*.[73] I will concern myself primarily with the type-type identities, and the philosophers in question will thus be immune to much of the discussion; but I will mention the other kinds of identities briefly.

Descartes, and others following him, argued that a person or mind is distinct from his body, since the mind could exist without the body. He might equally well have argued the same

[73] Thomas Nagel and Donald Davidson are notable examples. Their views are very interesting, and I wish I could discuss them in further detail. It is doubtful that such philosophers wish to call themselves 'materialists'. Davidson, in particular, bases his case for his version of the identity theory on the supposed *impossibility* of correlating psychological properties with physical ones.

The argument against token-token identification in the text *does* apply to these views.

conclusion from the premise that the body could have existed without the mind.[74] Now the one response which I regard as plainly inadmissible is the response which cheerfully accepts the Cartesian premise while denying the Cartesian conclusion. Let 'Descartes' be a name, or rigid designator, of a certain person, and let '*B*' be a rigid designator of his body. Then if Descartes were indeed identical to *B*, the supposed identity, being an identity between two rigid designators, would be necessary, and Descartes could not exist without *B* and *B* could not exist without Descartes. The case is not at all comparable to the alleged analogue, the identity of the first Postmaster General with the inventor of bifocals. True, this identity obtains despite the fact that there could have been a first Postmaster General even though bifocals had never been invented. The reason is that 'the inventor of bifocals' is not a rigid designator; a world in which no one invented bifocals is not *ipso facto* a world in which Franklin did not exist. The alleged analogy therefore collapses; a philosopher who wishes

[74] Of course, the body *does* exist without the mind and presumably without the person, when the body is a corpse. This consideration, if accepted, would already show that a person and his body are distinct. (See David Wiggins, 'On Being at the Same Place at the Same Time', *Philosophical Review*, Vol. 77 (1968), pp. 90–5.) Similarly, it can be argued that a statue is not the hunk of matter of which it is composed. In the latter case, however, one might say instead that the former is 'nothing over and above' the latter; and the same device might be tried for the relation of the person and the body. The difficulties in the text would not then arise in the same form, but analogous difficulties would appear. A theory that a person is nothing over and above his body in the way that a statue is nothing over and above the matter of which it is composed, would have to hold that (necessarily) a person exists if and only if his body exists and has a certain additional physical organization. Such a thesis would be subject to modal difficulties similar to those besetting the ordinary identity thesis, and the same would apply to suggested analogues replacing the identification of mental states with physical states. A further discussion of this matter must be left for another place. Another view which I will not discuss, although I have little tendency to accept it and am not even certain that it has been set out with genuine clarity, is the so-called functional state view of psychological concepts.

to refute the Cartesian conclusion must refute the Cartesian premise, and the latter task is not trivial.

Let '*A*' name a particular pain sensation, and let '*B*' name the corresponding brain state, or the brain state some identity theorist wishes to identify with *A*. *Prima facie*, it would seem that it is at least logically possible that *B* should have existed (Jones's brain could have been in exactly that state at the time in question) without Jones feeling any pain at all, and thus without the presence of *A*. Once again, the identity theorist cannot admit the possibility cheerfully and proceed from there; consistency, and the principle of the necessity of identities using rigid designators, disallows any such course. If *A* and *B* were identical, the identity would have to be necessary. The difficulty can hardly be evaded by arguing that although *B* could not exist without *A*, *being a pain* is merely a contingent property of *A*, and that therefore the presence of *B* without pain does not imply the presence of *B* without *A*. Can any case of essence be more obvious than the fact that *being a pain* is a necessary property of each pain? The identity theorist who wishes to adopt the strategy in question must even argue that *being a sensation* is a contingent property of *A*, for *prima facie* it would seem logically possible that *B* could exist without any sensation with which it might plausibly be identified. Consider a particular pain, or other sensation, that you once had. Do you find it at all plausible that *that very sensation* could have existed without being a sensation, the way a certain inventor (Franklin) could have existed without being an inventor?

I mention this strategy because it seems to me to be adopted by a large number of identity theorists. These theorists, believing as they do that the supposed identity of a brain state with the corresponding mental state is to be analyzed on the paradigm of the contingent identity of Benjamin Franklin with the inventor of bifocals, realize that just as his contingent activity made Benjamin Franklin into the inventor of bifocals, so some contingent property of the brain state must make it into a pain. Generally they wish this property to be one statable in physical or at least 'topic-neutral' language, so that the materialist cannot be accused of positing irreducible non-physical properties. A typical view is that *being a pain*, as a property of a physical state, is to be analyzed in terms of the 'causal role' of the state,[75] in terms of the characteristic stimuli (e.g., pinpricks) which cause it and the characteristic behavior it causes. I will not go into the details of such analyses, even though I usually find them faulty on specific grounds in addition to the general modal considerations I argue here. All I need to observe here is that the 'causal role' of the physical state is regarded by the theorists in question as a contingent property of the state, and thus it is supposed to be a contingent property of the state that it is a mental state at all, let alone that it is something as specific as a pain. To repeat, this notion seems to me self-evidently absurd. It amounts to the view that the *very pain I now have* could have existed without being a mental state at all.

I have not discussed the converse problem, which is closer to the original Cartesian consideration—namely, that just as it seems that the brain state could have existed without any pain, so it seems that the pain could have existed without the corresponding brain state. Note that *being a brain state* is evidently an essential property of *B* (the brain state). Indeed, even more is true: not only being a brain state, but even being a brain state of a specific type is an essential property of *B*. The configuration of brain cells whose presence at a given time constitutes the presence of *B* at that time is essential to *B*, and in its absence *B* would not have existed. Thus someone who

[75] For example, David Armstrong, *A Materialist Theory of the Mind*, London and New York, 1968, see the discussion review by Thomas Nagel, *Philosophical Review* **79** (1970), pp. 394–403; and David Lewis, 'An Argument for the Identity Theory', *The Journal of Philosophy*, pp. 17–25.

wishes to claim that the brain state and the pain are identical must argue that the pain $A$ could not have existed without a quite specific type of configuration of molecules. If $A = B$, then the identity of $A$ with $B$ is necessary, and any essential property of one must be an essential property of the other. Someone who wishes to maintain an identity thesis cannot simply *accept* the Cartesian intuitions that $A$ can exist without $B$, that $B$ can exist without $A$, that the correlative presence of anything with mental properties is merely contingent to $B$, and that the correlative presence of any specific physical properties is merely contingent to $A$. He must explain these intuitions away, showing how they are illusory. This task may not be impossible; we have seen above how some things which appear to be contingent turn out, on closer examination, to be necessary. The task, however, is obviously not child's play, and we shall see below how difficult it is.

The final kind of identity, the one which I said would get the closest attention, is the type-type sort of identity exemplified by the identification of pain with the stimulation of C-fibers. These identifications are supposed to be analogous with such scientific type-type identifications as the identity of heat with molecular motion, of water with hydrogen hydroxide, and the like. Let us consider, as an example, the analogy supposed to hold between the materialist identification and that of heat with molecular motion; both identifications identify two types of phenomena. The usual view holds that the identification of heat with molecular motion and of pain with the stimulation of C-fibers are both contingent. We have seen above that since 'heat' and 'molecular motion' are both rigid designators, the identification of the phenomena they name is necessary. What about 'pain' and 'C-fiber stimulation'? It should be clear from the previous discussion that 'pain' is a rigid designator of the type, or phenomenon, it designates: if something is a pain it is essentially so, and it seems absurd to suppose that pain could have been some phenomenon other than the one it is. The same holds for the term 'C-fiber stimulation', provided that 'C-fibers' is a rigid designator, as I will suppose here. (The supposition is somewhat risky, since I know virtually nothing about C-fibers, except that the stimulation of them is said to be correlated with pain.[76] The point is unimportant; if 'C-fibers' is not a rigid designator, simply replace it by one which is, or suppose it used as a rigid designator in the present context.) Thus the identity of pain with the stimulation of C-fibers, if true, must be *necessary*.

So far the analogy between the identification of heat with molecular motion and pain with the stimulation of C-fibers has not failed; it has merely turned out to be the opposite of what is usually thought—both, if true, must be necessary. This means that the identity theorist is committed to the view that there could not be a C-fiber stimulation which was not a pain nor a pain which was not a C-fiber stimulation. These consequences are certainly surprising and counterintuitive, but let us not dismiss the identity theorist too quickly. Can he perhaps show that the apparent possibility of pain not having turned out to be C-fiber stimulation, or of there being an instance of one of

[76] I have been surprised to find that at least one able listener took my use of such terms as 'correlated with', 'corresponding to', and the like as already begging the question against the identity thesis. The identity thesis, so he said, is not the thesis that pains and brain states are correlated, but rather that they are identical. Thus my entire discussion presupposes the anti-materialist position that I set out to prove. Although I was surprised to hear an objection which concedes so little intelligence to the argument, I have tried especially to avoid the term 'correlated' which seems to give rise to the objection. Nevertheless, to obviate misunderstanding, I shall explain my usage. Assuming, at least *arguendo*, that scientific discoveries have turned out so as not to refute materialism from the beginning, both the dualist and the identity theorist agree that there is a correlation or correspondence between mental states and physical states. The dualist holds that the 'correlation' relation in question is irreflexive; the identity theorist holds that it is simply a special case of the identity relation. Such terms as 'correlation' and 'correspondence' can be used neutrally without prejudging which side is correct.

the phenomena which is not an instance of the other, is an illusion of the same sort as the illusion that water might not have been hydrogen hydroxide, or that heat might not have been molecular motion? If so, he will have rebutted the Cartesian, not, as in the conventional analysis, by accepting his premise while exposing the fallacy of his argument, but rather by the reverse—while the Cartesian argument, given its premise of the contingency of the identification, is granted to yield its conclusion, the premise is to be exposed as superficially plausible but false.

Now I do not think it likely that the identity theorist will succeed in such an endeavor. I want to argue that, at least, the case cannot be interpreted as analogous to that of scientific identification of the usual sort, as exemplified by the identity of heat and molecular motion. What was the strategy used above to handle the apparent contingency of certain cases of the necessary *a posteriori*? The strategy was to argue that although the statement itself is necessary, someone could, *qualitatively* speaking, be in the same epistemic situation as the original, and in such a situation a *qualitatively* analogous statement could be false. In the case of identities between two rigid designators, the strategy can be approximated by a simpler one: Consider how the references of the designators are determined; if these coincide only contingently, it is this fact which gives the original statement its illusion of contingency. In the case of heat and molecular motion, the way these two paradigms work out is simple. When someone says, inaccurately, that heat might have turned out not to be molecular motion, what is true in what he says is that someone could have sensed a phenomenon in the same way we sense heat, that is, feels it by means of its production of the sensation we call 'the sensation of heat' (call it '*S*'), even though that phenomenon was not molecular motion. He means, additionally, that the planet might have been inhabited by creatures who did not get *S* when they were in the presence of molecular motion, though perhaps getting it in the presence of something else. Such creatures would be, in some qualitative sense, in the same epistemic situation as we are, they could use a rigid designator for the phenomenon that causes sensation *S* in them (the rigid designator could even be 'heat'), yet it would not be molecular motion (and therefore not heat!), which was causing the sensation.

Now can something be said analogously to explain away the feeling that the identity of pain and the stimulation of C-fibers, if it is a scientific discovery, could have turned out otherwise? I do not see that such an analogy is possible. In the case of the apparent possibility that molecular motion might have existed in the absence of heat, what seemed really possible is that molecular motion should have existed without being *felt as heat*, that is, it might have existed without producing the sensation *S*, the sensation of heat. In the appropriate sentient beings is it analogously possible that a stimulation of C-fibers should have existed without being felt as pain? If this is possible, then the stimulation of C-fibers can itself exist without pain, since for it to exist without being *felt as pain* is for it to exist without there *being any* pain. Such a situation would be in flat out contradiction with the supposed necessary identity of pain and the corresponding physical state, and the analogue holds for any physical state which might be identified with a corresponding mental state. The trouble is that the identity theorist does not hold that the physical state merely *produces* the mental state, rather he wishes the two to be identical and thus *a fortiori* necessarily co-occurrent. In the case of molecular motion and heat there is something, namely, the sensation of heat, which is an intermediary between the external phenomenon and the observer. In the mental-physical case no such intermediary is possible, since here the physical phenomenon is supposed to be identical with the internal phenomenon itself. Someone can be in the same epistemic situation as he would be if there were heat, even in the absence of heat, simply by feeling the sensation of heat; and even in the presence of heat, he can have the same evidence as he would have in the absence of heat simply by lacking the sensation $S$. No such possibility exists in the case of pain and other mental phenomena. To be in the same epistemic situation that would obtain if one had a pain *is* to have a pain; to be in the same epistemic situation that would obtain in the absence of a pain *is* not to have a pain. The apparent contingency of the connection between the mental state and the corresponding brain state thus cannot be explained by some sort of qualitative analogue as in the case of heat.

We have just analyzed the situation in terms of the notion of a qualitatively identical epistemic situation. The trouble is that the notion of an epistemic situation qualitatively identical to one in which the observer had a sensation $S$ simply *is* one in which the observer had that sensation. The same point can be made in terms of the notion of what picks out the reference of a rigid designator. In the case of the identity of heat with molecular motion the important consideration was that although 'heat' is a rigid designator, the reference of that designator was determined by an accidental property of the referent, namely the property of producing in us the sensation $S$. It is thus possible that a phenomenon should have been rigidly designated in the same way as a phenomenon of heat, with its reference also picked out by means of the sensation $S$, without that phenomenon being heat and therefore without its being molecular motion. Pain, on the other hand, is not picked out by one of its accidental properties; rather it is picked out by the property of being pain itself, by its immediate phenomenological quality. Thus pain, unlike heat, is not only rigidly designated by 'pain' but the reference of the designator is determined by an essential property of the referent. Thus it is not possible to say that although pain is necessarily identical with a certain physical state, a certain phenomenon can be picked out in the same way we pick out pain without being correlated with that physical state. If any phenomenon is picked out in exactly the same way that we pick out pain, then that phenomenon *is* pain.

Perhaps the same point can be made more vivid without such specific reference to the technical apparatus in these lectures. Suppose we imagine God creating the world; what does He need to do to make the identity of heat and molecular motion obtain? Here it would seem that all He needs to do is to create the heat, that is, the molecular motion itself. If the air molecules on this earth are sufficiently agitated, if there is a burning fire, then the earth will be hot even if there are no observers to see it. God created light (and thus created streams of photons, according to present scientific doctrine) before He created human and animal observers; and the same presumably holds for heat. How then does it appear to us that the identity of molecular motion with heat is a substantive scientific fact, that the mere creation of molecular motion still leaves God with the additional task of making molecular motion into heat? This feeling is indeed illusory, but what *is* a substantive task for the Deity is the task of making molecular motion felt as heat. To do this He must create some sentient beings to insure that the molecular motion produces the sensation *S* in them. Only after he has done this will there be beings who can learn that the sentence 'Heat is the motion of molecules' expresses an *a posteriori* truth in precisely the same way that we do.

What about the case of the stimulation of C-fibers? To create this phenomenon, it would seem that God need only create beings with C-fibers capable of the appropriate type of physical stimulation; whether the beings are conscious or not is irrelevant here. It would seem, though, that to make the C-fiber stimulation correspond to pain, or be felt as pain, God must do something in addition to the mere creation of the C-fiber stimulation; He must let the creatures feel the C-fiber stimulation as *pain*, and not as a tickle, or as warmth, or as nothing, as apparently would also have been within His powers. If these things in fact are within His powers, the relation between the pain God creates and the stimulation of C-fibers cannot be identity. For if so, the stimulation could exist without the pain; and since 'pain' and 'C-fiber stimulation' are rigid, this fact implies that the relation between the two phenomena is not that of identity. God had to do some work, in addition to making the man himself, to make a certain man be the inventor of bifocals; the man could well exist without inventing any such thing. The same cannot be said for pain; if the phenomenon exists at all, no further work should be required to make it into pain.

In sum, the correspondence between a brain state and a mental state seems to have a certain obvious element of contingency. We have seen that identity is not a relation which can hold contingently between objects. Therefore, if the identity thesis were correct, the element of contingency would not lie in the relation between the mental and physical states. It cannot lie, as in the case of heat and molecular motion, in the relation between the phenomenon (= heat = molecular motion) and the way it is felt or appears (sensation *S*), since in the case of mental phenomena there is no 'appearance' beyond the mental phenomenon itself.

Here I have been emphasizing the possibility, or apparent possibility, of a physical state without the corresponding mental state. The reverse possibility, the mental state (pain) without the physical state (C-fiber stimulation) also presents problems for the identity theorists which cannot be resolved by appeal to the analogy of heat and molecular motion.

I have discussed similar problems more briefly for views equating the self with the body, and particular mental events with particular physical events, without discussing possible countermoves in the same detail as in the type-type case. Suffice it to say that I suspect that the considerations given indicate that the theorist who wishes to identify various particular mental and physical events will have to face problems fairly similar to those of the type-type theorist; he too will be unable to appeal to the standard alleged analogues.

That the usual moves and analogies are not available to solve the problems of the identity theorist is, of course, no proof that no moves are available. I certainly cannot discuss all the possibilities here. I suspect, however, that the present considerations tell heavily against the usual forms of materialism. Materialism, I think, must hold that a physical description of the world is a *complete* description of it, that any mental facts are 'ontologically dependent' on physical facts in the straightforward sense of following from them by necessity. No identity theorist seems to me to have made a convincing argument against the intuitive view that this is not the case.[77]

[77] Having expressed these doubts about the identity theory in the text, I should emphasize two things: first, identity theorists have presented positive arguments for their view, which I certainly have not answered here. Some of these arguments seem to me to be weak or based on ideological prejudices, but others strike me as highly compelling arguments which I am at present unable to answer convincingly. Second, rejection of the identity thesis does not imply acceptance of Cartesian dualism. In fact, my view above that a person could not have come from a different sperm and egg from the ones from which he actually originated implicitly suggests a rejection of the Cartesian picture. If we had a clear idea of the soul or the mind as an independent, susbsistent, spiritual entity, why should it have to have any necessary connection with particular material objects such as a particular sperm or a particular egg? A convinced dualist may think that my views on sperms and eggs beg the question against Descartes. I would tend to argue the other way; the fact that it is hard to imagine me coming from a sperm and egg different from my actual origins seems to me to indicate that we have no such clear conception of a soul or self. In any event, Descartes' notion seems to have been rendered dubious ever since Hume's critique of the notion of a Cartesian self. I regard the mind-body problem as wide open and extremely confusing.

# ADDENDA

These addenda represent certain amplifications of the original text which I have added either in response to questions or for the sake of clarification or sketchy amplification.

(a) *Unicorns*, pp. 23–4. In the light of the remarks on natural kinds made in the third lecture, I shall try to give a brief explanation of the strange view of unicorns advocated in the text. There were two theses: first, a *metaphysical* thesis that no counterfactual situation is properly describable as one in which there would have been unicorns; second, an *epistemological* thesis that an archeological discovery that there were animals with all the features attributed to unicorns in the appropriate myth would not in and of itself constitute proof that there were unicorns.

As to the metaphysical thesis, the argument basically is the following. Just as tigers are an actual species, so the unicorns are a mythical species. Now tigers, as I argue in the third lecture, cannot be defined simply in terms of their appearance; it is possible that there should have been a different species with all the external appearances of tigers but which had a different internal structure and therefore was not the species of tigers. We may be misled into thinking otherwise by the fact that actually no such 'fool's tigers' exist, so that in practice external appearance is sufficient to identify the species. Now there is no actual species of unicorns, and regarding the several distinct hypothetical species, with different internal structures (some reptilic, some mammalian, some amphibious), which would have the external appearances postulated to hold of unicorns in the myth of the unicorn, one cannot say which of these distinct mythical species would have *been* the unicorns. If we suppose, as I do, that the unicorns of the myth were supposed to be a particular species, but that the myth provides insufficient information about their internal structure to determine a unique species, then there is no actual or possible species of which we can say that it would have been the species of unicorns.

The epistemological thesis is more easily argued. If a story is found describing a substance with the physical appearance of gold, one cannot conclude on this basis that it is talking about gold; it may be talking about 'fools' gold'. What substance is being discussed must be determined as in the case of proper names: by the historical connection of the story with a certain substance. When the connection is traced, it may well turn out that the substance dealt with was gold, 'fools' gold', or something else. Similarly, the mere discovery of animals with the properties attributed to unicorns in the myth would by no means show that these were the animals the myth was about: perhaps the myth was spun out of whole cloth, and the fact that animals with the same appearance actually existed was mere coincidence. In that case, we cannot say that the unicorns of the myth really existed; we must also establish a historical connection that shows that the myth is *about* these animals.

I hold similar views regarding fictional proper names. The mere discovery that there was indeed a detective with exploits like those of Sherlock Holmes would not show that Conan Doyle was writing *about* this man; it is theoretically possible, though in practice fantastically unlikely, that Doyle was writing pure fiction with only a coincidental resemblance to the actual man. (See the characteristic disclaimer: 'The characters in this work are fictional, and any resemblance to anyone, living or dead, is purely coincidental.') Similarly, I hold the metaphysical view that, granted that there is no Sherlock Holmes, one cannot say of any possible person that he *would have been* Sherlock Holmes, had he existed. Several distinct possible people, and even actual ones such as Darwin or Jack the Ripper, might have performed the exploits of Holmes, but there is none of whom we can say that he would have *been* Holmes had he performed these exploits. For if so, which one?

I thus could no longer write, as I once did, that 'Holmes does not exist, but in other states of affairs, he would have existed.' (See my 'Semantical Considerations on Modal Logic', *Acta Philosophica Fennica*, Vol. **16** (1963) pp. 83–94; reprinted in L. Linsky (ed.), *Reference and Modality*, Oxford University Press, (1971; p. 65 in the Linsky reprint.) The quoted assertion gives the erroneous impression that a fictional name such as 'Holmes' names a particular possible-but-not-actual individual. The substantive point I was trying to make, however, remains and is independent of any linguistic theory of the status of names in fiction. The point was that, in other possible worlds 'some actually existing individuals may be absent while new individuals . . . may appear' (*ibid*, p. 65), and that if in an open formula $A(x)$ the free variable is assigned a given individual as value, a problem arises as to whether (in a model-theoretic treatment of modal logic) a truth-value is to be assigned to the formula in worlds in which the individual in question does not exist.

I am aware that the cryptic brevity of these remarks diminishes whatever persuasiveness they may otherwise possess. I expect to elaborate on them elsewhere, in a forthcoming work discussing the problems of existential statements, empty names, and fictional entities.

(b) *Can to must*, first paragraph of p. 35. An unpublished paper by Barry T. Stroud has called my attention to the fact that Kant himself makes a closely related mistake. Kant says, 'Experience teaches us that a thing is so and so, but not that it cannot be otherwise. First, then, if we have a proposition which in being thought is thought as *necessary*, it is an *a priori* judgement. . . . Necessity and strict universality are thus sure criteria of *a priori* knowledge'. (*Critique of Pure Reason* B3–4, pp. 43–4 in the Kemp Smith translation, Macmillan, 1956.) Kant thus appears to hold that if a proposition is known to be *necessary*, the mode of knowledge not only *can* be *a priori* but *must* be. On the contrary, one can learn a mathematical truth *a posteriori* by consulting a computing machine, or even by asking a mathematician. Nor can Kant argue that experience can tell us that a mathematical proposition is *true*, but not that it is *necessary*; for the peculiar character of mathematical propositions (like Goldbach's conjecture) is that one knows (*a priori*) that they cannot be contingently true; a mathematical statement, if true, is necessary.

All the cases of the necessary *a posteriori* advocated in the text have the special character attributed to mathematical statements: Philosophical analysis tells us that they cannot be contingently true, so any empirical knowledge of their truth is automatically empirical knowledge that they are necessary. This characterization applies, in particular, to the cases of identity statements and of essence. It *may* give a clue to a general characterization of *a posteriori* knowledge of necessary truths.

I should mention that if the possibility of knowing a mathematical truth by consulting a computer were the only objection to Kant offered, it would still be open to him to hold: (1) that every necessary truth is knowable *a priori*; or, more weakly, (2) that every necessary truth, if known at all, must be knowable *a priori*. Both (1) and (2) involve the obscure notion of the *possibility* of *a priori* knowledge, but to the extent that the notion is clarified by restricting it to *a priori* knowledge of a standard human sort, I argue against both (1) and (2) in the text. In fact, of course, I hold that propositions that contemporary philosophers would properly count as 'empirical' can be necessary and be known to be such.

Perhaps I should mention also that I have been unable to find the characterization of *a priori* truth as truth which *can* be known independently of experience in Kant; as far as I can see, Kant refers only to *a priori* knowledge of particular statements, which does not involve the extra modality. (In the text, I incautiously ascribed this common characterization of *a priori* truth to Kant.) And, of course, when Kant uses 'necessary' for a type of proposition and '*a priori*' for a mode of knowledge he cannot possibly be guilty of the common contemporary practice of treating the two terms as interchangeable synonyms. It is clear from the opening pages of the *Critique* that he regards the thesis that knowledge that something is necessary must be *a priori* knowledge as an important, though obvious, substantive thesis.

(c) Some remarks that I have heard lead me to suppose that the noncircularity condition could use further clarification. First, my remark on p. 68 has been misunderstood to say that a definition such as 'Jonah is the man referred to by that name in the Bible' necessarily violates the noncircularity condition. It does not, provided that the description theory can give an account of the Biblical authors' reference which is independent of our own. When I discuss Strawson, I explicitly acknowledge that a speaker may use a description of this sort which 'passes the buck' and that the procedure is noncircular provided that the other speaker's description does not ultimately involve the references made by the original speaker. Thus I can say, 'Let "Glumph" be a name of the thing Jones calls "Glumph" ', provided that Jones does not simultaneously say, 'Let "Glumph" be a name of the thing Kripke calls "Glumph".'

The objection to such noncircular determinations of reference as 'Let "Glumph" be the man Jones calls "Glumph"' and, 'Let Gödel be the man to whom the experts attribute the incompleteness theorem' (said by a layman) is otherwise: In general, a speaker cannot be sure from whom he picked up his reference; and as far as he knows 'the experts' may well realize that Schmidt, not Gödel, proved the incompleteness theorem even though the inexpert speaker still attributes it to Gödel. Thus such determinations of the referent may well give the wrong result, and the speaker surely cannot be said to know *a priori* (as in Thesis 5) that they do not. (See my criticisms of Strawson in the text.) If, on the other hand, the speaker attempts to avoid the possibility of such error by using his *own* reference as the paradigm, as in such determinations as 'Let Glumph be the man *I* call "Glumph" (now)' or 'Let Gödel be the man I believe to have proved the incompleteness theorem,' the determination of the reference *is* circular (unless the speaker has already determined his reference in some other way, in which case that is the determining condition and not the one stated). Often the determination of the reference risks falling afoul both of circularity *and* of vulnerability to error, for the speaker may not know whether those others to whom he 'passes the buck' may not in turn pass the buck to him. Blatant cases of vulnerability to both types of criticisms is to be found in such determinations as, 'Let "Glumph" denote the man all of us in Community *C* call "Glumph",' or 'Let "Gödel" denote the man presently generally believed in Community *C* to have proved the incompleteness theorem,' if this determination is supposed to be the one used throughout Community *C*. For an individual speaker may err in such a determination if the community in general has been apprised of the Gödel-Schmidt fraud but the speaker has not; and even if the possibility of error is waived, the determination will be circular if it is supposed that all, or even the large majority, of the speakers of Community *C* use it to determine their reference.

All these points are stated in the text, but misunderstandings have led me to believe that a summary restatement could conceivably do some good. Quite a different way of determining the reference would be, 'Let "Glumph" denote the man called "Glumph" by the people from whom I got it (whoever they are), provided that my present determination of the reference satisfies the conditions sketched in "Naming and Necessity" and whatever other conditions need be satisfied'. As I said in footnote 38, such a determination would constitute a trivial fulfillment of the description theory in terms of the present view if only the present view were not somewhat loose and did not already involve the notion of the speaker's own reference (in terms of his intention to agree in reference with those from whom he picked up the name). Even if both these problems were surmounted, the resulting description would hardly be one of the type which occurs to a speaker when he is asked such a question as, 'Who is Napoleon?', as the description theorists intended. It would occur only to those speakers who have mastered a complex theory of reference, and it would be this theory, of course, and not the speaker's knowledge of a description, which gave the true picture of how the reference was determined.

(d) *Initial 'baptism'*, p. 96. In footnote 70 on natural kind terms, I mention that the notion of an initial sample appealed to there gives an oversimplified picture of the case. Analogously for proper names, of course I recognize that there need not always be an identifiable initial baptism; so the picture is oversimplified. Of course I also think, analogously to footnote 70, that such complications will not radically alter the picture. It is probably true, however, that in the case of proper names, examples with no identifiable initial baptism are rarer than in the species case.

(e) *Santa Claus*, p. 93 and pp. 96–7. Gareth Evans has pointed out that similar cases of reference shifts arise where the shift is not from a real entity to a fictional one, but from one real entity to another of the same kind. According to Evans, 'Madagascar' was a native name for a part of Africa; Marco Polo, erroneously thinking that he was following native usage, applied the name to an island. (Evans uses the example to support the description theory; I, of course, do not.) Today the usage of the name as a name for an island has become so widespread that it surely overrides any historical connection with the native name. David Lewis has pointed out that the same thing could have happened even if the natives had used 'Madagascar' to designate a mythical locality. So real reference can shift to another real reference, fictional reference can shift to real, and real to fictional. In all these cases, a present intention to refer to a given entity (or to refer fictionally) overrides the original intention to preserve reference in the historical chain of transmission. The matter deserves extended discussion. But the phenomenon is perhaps roughly explicable in terms of the predominantly social character of the use of proper names emphasized in the text: we use names to communicate with other speakers in a common language. This character dictates ordinarily that a speaker intend to use a name the same way as it was transmitted to him; but in the 'Madagascar' case this social character dictates that the present intention to refer to an island overrides the distant link to native usage. (Probably Miller's case, 'George Smith' vs. 'Newton' is similarly explicable.) To state all this with any precision undoubtedly requires more apparatus than I have developed here; in particular, we must distinguish a present intention to use a name for an object from a mere present belief that the object is the only one having a certain property, and clarify this distinction. I leave the problem for further work.

(f) I perhaps should mention (amplifying p. 23 n. 2) that

the historical acquisition picture of naming advocated here is apparently very similar to views of Keith Donnellan. (Charles Chastain also made similar suggestions, but they had a greater admixture of the old description theory.) David Kaplan's investigation of 'Dthat', mentioned in footnote 22, has been extended to a 'logic of demonstratives' in which, he says, a good deal of the argument of this paper can be given a formal representation. Indeed a good deal of this paper suggests a certain formal apparatus, though the present presentation is informal.

(g) The third lecture suggests that a good deal of what contemporary philosophy regards as mere physical necessity is actually necessary *tout court*. The question how far this can be pushed is one I leave for further work.

# INDEX

Albritton, Rogers, 23n, 122n
Alpha Centauri, 95
Analytic truth, 34, 39, 56n, 117, 122, 135
*A posteriori* truth, *see A priori* truth, Necessary *a posteriori* truth
*A priori* truth (a prioricity), as epistemological notion, 34–9, 63, 122–3, 158–60; Kant's views on, 34, 117, 158–60; *see also* Contingent *a priori* truth, Necessary *a posteriori* truth
Aristotle, 6–14, 29–30, 57, 61–3, 65, 74–5
Armstrong, David, 147n
Atomic number, 116, 123–5, 138, 140; *see also* Gold
Attribute, 138

'Baptism', initial, 78, 96–7, 106, 135–40, 162
'Bare particulars', 18, 52
Bifocals, the inventor of, 98, 145–6, 154
Brain state, *see* Mind-body identity thesis

Cartesian dualism, 155n
Catiline, 79–81
Cats, 122–3, 125–6, 134
Causal chain (in reference), *see* Chain of communication
Causal role (of mental states), 147
Certainty, 34, 39
C-fibers, 98, 144, 148–54
Chain of communication (in reference), 8n, 59n, 91–7, 106, 116n, 135, 139, 157, 163–4; and shift of reference, 93–7, 163–4
Chastain, Charles, 23n, 164
Cicero, 20, 79–81, 92, 97n, 98, 100–1, 107–8
Cluster concept, 55n, 60, 76, 120–1, 122n
'Cluster of descriptions' theory of proper names, *see* Description theory of proper names
Columbus, C., 85
Connotation (Mill), 26, 127, 134
Contingent *a priori* truth, 14–15, 54–7, 63, 66, 75–6, 78–9, 80–91 *passim*, 96n, 135–8; *see also* Fixing the reference of a term, Rigid designators

Correlation (of the physical with the mental), 98–9, 144n, 149n
Count noun, 134; *see also* Natural kinds
Counterpart Theory, 45, 51n, 76–7, 142
Cows, 127–8
Criterion of identity, *see* Identity

Dali, Salvador, 32
Dartmouth, 26
Davidson, Donald, 144n
Dedekind, R., 84–5, 88–9
Definite description(s), alleged 'rigid' sense of, 6n, 59n; referent of, 24–6, 86n; 'referential' use of, 7n, 25, 59n, 80n, 85n, 87n; relation to proper names, *see* Description theory of proper names; and scope distinctions, 10–14, 59n, 61–2
Definition, qualitative, 122; two senses of, 54–60, 123n, 134–6, 140n; *see also* Contingent *a priori* truth, Fixing the reference of a term
Demons, 122, 126
Demonstratives, 10n, 27n, 49n, 101, 164
Denotation (Mill), 26, 134
Descartes, R., 144–5, 155n
Description theory of proper names, 'cluster' version distinguished, 30–2, 60–1, 74, 134–5; non-circularity condition on, 68–73, 88n, 89–90, 160–2; as theory of meaning, 5–15, 27–34, 53–77, 127, 134–135; theory of meaning distinct from theory of reference, 5, 15, 32–4, 53–78 *passim*, 79n, 96n, 97n, 106–7; as theory of reference only, 57–8, 66–8, 78–97, 106–7
Designator, 24; non-rigid (accidental), 48, *see also* Rigid designators; rigid, *see* Rigid designators; strongly rigid, 48–9
Determine the reference (referent) of a term, 27–34, 53–164 *passim*; *see also* Fixing the reference of a term
Donnellan, Keith, 7n, 23n, 25, 59n, 80n, 85n, 87n, 164
Doyle, A. Conan, 157
'Dthat', 60n, 164
Dualism, *see* Mind-body identity thesis; Cartesian, 155n
Dummett, Michael, 11n

Einstein, A., 81–3, 87, 95
Electricity, 116, 132, 136
Electromagnetic radiation, 98, 129
Element, 116, 118, 124; *see also* Gold
Elizabeth II, 110–13, 141
Epistemic contexts, 20–1
Epistemic situation, qualitatively identical, 103–5, 141–4, 150–3
Epistemology, epistemological notion, *see A priori* truth, Necessary *a posteriori* truth
Essence, 47, 77, 115n, 126, 138, 141, 146; *see also* Essential properties
Essential properties, of individuals, 39–53, 110–15, 126–7,

140–2, 155n; of natural kinds and phenomena, 123–6, 128–157 *passim*; of sensations, 146–155
Essentialism, meaningfulness of, 39–53; *see also* Essential properties
Evans, Gareth, 163
Everest, 100
Existential statements, 29, 31–3, 58–9, 65–7, 110

Fermat's Last Theorem, 36, 141, 143
Feynman, Richard, 81–2, 91–2
Fictional entities, 157–8, 163; *see also* Legendary characters, Santa Claus, Unicorns
Fixing the reference (referent) of a term, distinct from giving a synonym, 15, 53–60, 61–164 *passim*; and mental terms, *see* Pain; and natural kinds, 122, 135–6, 139, 162; and natural phenomena, 130–4, 136–7, 139–40, 148–55; and proper names, *see* Description theory of proper names, Proper names; *see also* Contingent *a priori* truth, Meter, π, Rigid designators, Yard, Yellow
Fool's gold, *see* Iron pyrites
Four color theorem, the, 103
Franklin, Benjamin, 145–6; *see also* Bifocals, the inventor of
Frege, Gottlob, 5, 27–31, 53–4, 58–60, 88n, 107, 127, 128n, 134–5
Functional state theory (of psychological concepts), 145n

Gaurisanker, 100
Geach, Peter, 23n, 115n
Gell-Mann, Murray 81, 91
General term, 127–8, 134–40; *see also* Natural kinds, Natural phenomena
Gilbert, Margaret, 1
Ginsberg, H. L., 67n
'Glumph', 'Glunk', 73, 160–2
God, 26–7, 153–4
Gödel, K., 37, 83–92, 161
Gold, 39, 116–19, 123–5, 127, 134–40, 142–3, 157; fool's, *see* Iron pyrites
Goldbach's conjecture, 36–8, 159

Hadleyburg, the man who corrupted, 24, 28
Heat, 98–9, 129, 131–4, 136, 138, 140, 148–54
Henry I, 76
Hesperus, 20, 28–9, 57–8, 78–9, 94, 98, 100–5, 108–10, 116n
Hilbert, D., 37
Historical connection (of term with referent), *see* Chain of communication
Hitler, A., 75, 77–8
$H_2O$, 99, 116, 128–9, 134, 148, 150; *see also* Water
Holmes, Sherlock, 157–8
Holy Roman Empire, The, 26
Humphrey, H., 45n, 48–9

Identifying marks (properties) of a natural kind, original, 118–122, 124–6, 128–9, 137–8, 156
Identity, 'across possible worlds', *see* 'Transworld identification'; criterion of, 17, 42–53, 115n;

Identity—*cont.*
  and Leibnitz's law, 3; necessary and sufficient conditions for, 43, 46–7, 50–2; necessity of, 3–5, 97–105, 107–110, 114n, 128–38, 140–55; of properties, 138; as a relation, 3–4, 107–8; over time, 43, 50–52, 115n; transitivity of, 51n; type-type, *see* Mind-body identity thesis; and vagueness, 50–1
Identity statements, 3–5, 28–9, 33, 66, 97–105, 107–10, 116, 128–36, 138, 140–1, 143–55
Identity thesis, *see* Mind-body identity thesis
Indiscernibility of identicals, 3
Intention, role of in preserving reference, *see* Chain of communication
Internal structure (of members of species), 120–1, 126, 156–7
Iron pyrites (fool's gold), 119, 124, 134, 135n, 136, 157

Jack the Ripper, 79, 94
Jacobson, Anne, 8n
'Joe Doakes', 28
Jonah, 67–8, 87, 160

Kant, Immanuel, 34, 39, 117, 123n, 134, 158–60
Kaplan, David, 10n, 45n, 60n, 164
Kinetic energy (of molecules), *see* Temperature
Kneale, William, 68–70, 72

Legendary characters, 66–7; *see also* Fictional entities
Leibnitz, G., 45n
Leibnitz's law, 3
Leverrier, U. J. J., 79n
Lewis, David K., 45, 51n, 76, 147n, 163
Light, 98–9, 116, 126–31, 134, 139, 153
Lightning, 116, 132, 134
Linsky, Leonard, 25n
Lockwood, Michael, 20n

Madagascar, 163
Marcus, Ruth Barcan, 100–1
Mass term, 127, 134; *see also* Gold, Water
Materialism, 23, 144n, 147–8, 155; *see also* Mind-body identity thesis
Mental state (property, event), *see* Mind-body identity thesis
Metal, concept of, 117–18; *see also* Gold, Natural kinds
Metaphysical notion, *see* Necessity, Necessary *a posteriori* truth
Meter, 54–6, 63, 75–6, 96n, 107, 135
Mill, John Stuart, 20, 26–8, 127–128, 134–5
Miller, Richard, 95n, 163
Mind-body identity thesis, 23, 98–100, 144–55; and Cartesian dualism, 155n; concerning particular states, 144, 146–8; concerning person and body, 144–6; concerning types of state, 144, 148–55
Mind-body problem, 23, 155n; *see also* Mind-body identity thesis

Modality *de re*, see Essential properties; scepticism about, 39–53
Modal logic, *see* Possible worlds
Molecular motion, 98–9, 129, 131–3, 138, 148–54
Moses, 31, 33–4, 58–9, 61, 65–7
Mythical entities, 24, 156–7, 163; *see also* Fictional entities, Legendary characters

Nagel, Thomas, 144n, 147n
Name, 'common name', 127; 'general name' (Mill), 127, 134; proper, *see* Proper names; 'singular name' (Mill), 127, 134; *see also* Natural kinds, Natural phenomena
'Nancy', 116n
Napoleon, 28, 96, 162
Nations, relation to individuals, 50
Natural kinds, 116–29, 134–44, 156–7, 162; *see also* Essential properties, Fixing the reference of a term; *also* Gold, Tigers, *etc.*
Natural phenomena, 98, 116, 129–40, 148–55; *see also* Essential properties, Fixing the reference of a term; *also* Heat, Light
Necessary *a posteriori* truth, 35–8, 158–60; and essential properties of individuals, 47, 49–50, 110–15, 126–7, 140–2; and identity statements between names, 100–5, 107–10, 140–4; and mathematics, 35–8, 103, 141, 143, 159–60; and mind-body identity thesis, 144–55; and natural kinds and natural phenomena, 122–6, 128–34, 137–8, 140–55; and qualitatively identical epistemic situation, 103–5, 141–4, 150–3
Necessary property, *see* Essential properties
Necessity, 3–5, 34–57, 58–78 *passim*, 97–115, 122–60, 164; of composition, 47, 50–3, 113–115, 126–7, 141–2; *de re, see* Essential properties, Modality *de re*; of identity, *see* Identity; logical, 35, 41; as a metaphysical notion, 34–9, 122–3, 135, 158–60; of origin, 110–115, 140–2, 155n; physical, 35, 99, 125, 164; *see also* Contingent *a priori* truth, Necessary *a posteriori* truth
Neptune, 79n, 96n
Newton, Isaac, 95, 97, 163
Nine, number, 40, 48
Nixon, Richard, 40–9, 51–3, 115n
Nozick, Robert, 88n

Onassis, Aristotle, 8–9
Optical illusion, and gold, 118; and tigers, 120–1
Origin, necessity of, 110–15, 115n, 140–2
Ostension, 28, 96–7, 115n, 135; *see also* 'Baptism', initial, Demonstratives

$\pi$, 60
Pain, 98–9, 144, 146–55
Peano, G., 84–5, 88–9
Person, and identity with body,

Person—*cont.*
144–6; *see also* Mind-body identity thesis
Phosphorus (planet), 20, 28–9, 80n, 98, 100–5, 108–10
Photons, 98–9, 116, 129, 130, 132, 153
Physical phenomena, *see* Natural phenomena
Polywater, 129
Possible but non-actual individuals, 158
Possible worlds, 1–164 *passim*; and the actual world, 16–20, 113, 115n; correct and incorrect conceptions of, 15–20, 43–53, 76; identity 'across', *see* 'Transworld identification'; and probability, 16–20; and semantics for modal logic, 3, 15n, 19n, 43, 48n, 59n, 158; stipulated, not discovered, 44, 49
Postmaster General of the Unites States, first, 98–9, 145
Proper names, correct picture of reference of, 91–7, 98–164 *passim*; description theory of, *see* Description theory of proper names; in epistemic contexts, 20–1; in fiction and legend, 66–7, 93, 96–7, 157–8, 163; 'homonymous', 7–10; and identity statements, *see* Identity, necessity of; as rigid designators, *see* Rigid designators; and scope distinctions, 10–14, 61–2; shift of reference of, 93–7, 163–4; and sortals, 115n; and terms for natural kinds and natural phenomena, 127–8, 134–5, 162; *see also under individual proper names*
Properties, contingent (accidental) used to fix reference, *see* Contingent *a priori* truth, Fixing the reference of a term; dispositional, 140n; essential, *see* Essentialism, Essential properties; mental and physical, *see* Mind-body identity thesis; necessary, *see* Essentialism, Essential properties; 'pure', 128n; used originally to identify a natural kind, 118–22, 124–6, 128–9, 137–8, 156
Psychophysical identification, *see* Mind-body identity thesis
Putnam, Hilary, 23n, 122–3, 125

*Quale*, 128; *see also* Mind-body identity thesis
Qualities, primary and secondary, 140
Quantified modal logic, *see* Possible worlds
Quantum mechanics, 45n
Queen, the, 110–13, 141
Quine, W. V., 29n, 40, 100–1

Referent, of a description, 24–6, 86n; of a proper name, *see* Description theory, Proper names; semantic, 25n; *see also* Fixing the reference of a term
Referential-attributive distinction, 7n, 25n, 59n, 80n 85n, 87n

Rigid designators, 3–15, 48–9, 55–60, 61–164 *passim*; and alleged 'ambiguity' of definite descriptions, 6n, 59n; and contingent existence, 3, 48–9, 109–10; *de jure* and *de facto*, 21n; demonstratives as, 10n, 49n; and identity statements, *see* Identity, necessity of; and the mind-body identity thesis, 144–55 *passim*; proper names as, 4–15, 48–53, 57–63, 74–6, 102–10; and scope distinctions, 10–14, 59n, 61–2; and terms for natural kinds and phenomena, 116–55 *passim*; variables as, 49n; *see also* Fixing the reference of a term
Rosser, J. B., 107
Russell, Bertrand, 5–14, 20, 27–31, 53–4, 58–60, 62, 70, 72, 87n, 88n, 97n, 101, 127, 134–5

Salmon, Nathan, 1n
Sample, initial (of a substance), 135–6, 138–9, 162
Santa Claus, 93, 97, 163
'Schmidentity', 108
'Schmidt', 84–91, 161
Scope distinction, 10–14, 59n, 61–2
Scott, Walter, 27n, 28, 32, 70
Searle, John R., 31, 61, 74–5
Self, 154, 155n; *see also* Person
Sensations, *see* Heat, Mind-body identity thesis, Pain, Yellow
Sense, Fregean, 27, 30, 59, 134
Singular term, *see* Definite description, General term, Name, Proper name
Slote, Michael, 23n, 115
'Smith, George', 95–7, 163
Socrates, 29n, 68–70, 72–3
Sortal, 115n
Sound, 98, 130, 133n, 134
Species, *see* Natural kinds; mythical, *see* Unicorns
Sprigge, Timothy, 110–11
Stalnaker, Robert, 20n
Strawson, P. F., 61, 65, 88n, 90, 92–3, 160–1
Stroud, Barry T., 158
Substance, *see* Natural kinds, Gold, Water
Substitutivity (of proper names), 20–1
Synonymy, *see* Contingent *a priori* truth, Fixing the reference of a term

Table (composition of), 47, 50–53, 113–15, 126–7, 141–2
Temperature, 129; *see also* Heat; boiling temperature of water, 54–6, 96n
Theoretical identification, 98–100, 116, 128–43; and mind-body identity thesis, 148–55
Tigers, 119–21, 127, 134, 137–8, 156–7
'Topic-neutral' language, 147
'Transworld identification', 15–20, 42–53, 76–7
Tully, 20, 98, 100–1, 107–8; *see also* Cicero
Twain, Mark, 113
Type-type identity (and mind-body identity thesis), 144, 148–55

Unicorns, 24, 157–8
United Nations, The, 26

Venus, 28, 100–5; *see also* Hesperus

Water, boiling temperature of, 54–6, 96n; molecular structure of, 99, 116, 126–9, 134, 148, 150
Whales, 138
Wiggins, David, 3, 145n
Wittgenstein, Ludwig, 31, 33, 54, 66

Yard, 76
Yellow, 118–19, 128n, 134, 140n

Ziff, Paul, 32, 80, 119–20